Born In Fo

Laila Bhimani

Table of Contents

Dedication

This book is dedicated in the memory of Suleiman, Fatema's brother who died in a tragic accident at the age of fourteen. May Lord rest his soul in peace, AMEN!

The proceedings will go to charity called Shelter for Homeless People. After what Fatema's son Arif went through made her realise that his father ruined Arif's career prospects by admitting him to a Psychiatric Hospital and forcing prescription drugs to him, Fatema is convinced that 'bad parenting' is the cause of so many young people on the streets today.

In 2016, Fatema wrote to Theresa May on Facebook to seek for the very wealthy to help donate; that is where help is needed.

Fatema wrote to Forbes to request the wealthiest to donate as Inheritance Tax of 40% goes to Tax man; it's best to donate to the homeless young people to give them some kind of future to our future generation.

Some people survive chaos

And that is how they grow.

And some people thrive in chaos,

Because chaos is all they know.

'Via Pinterest'

Acknowledgements

Fatema would like to thank Mustafa for his encouragement and moral support in the development of this book. Mustafa was a neighbour in Uganda and a close friend of Fatema's deceased brother Suleiman. May Lord rest his soul in peace, Amen.

"He who has gone, so we but cherish his memory, abides with us, more potent, nay, more present than the living man." — Antoine de Saint-Exupery

About the Author

This is an autobiography, a true story set in Uganda. The author has narrated the book in third person to conceal the identity of her family.

Preface

This true story is set in Uganda, East Africa. The characters and some of the locations are fictitious to conceal the identity of the author's family. The author is a Ugandan Asian born in Fort Portal, the most scenic and the best part of the country. Uganda is known as the Pearl of Africa. Its physical features, such as Murchison Falls National Park and Hot Springs near Fort Portal, and many other breath-taking attractions are not to be missed.

She fled the country in November 1972 when Idi Amin expelled all the Asians from Uganda. She recently visited the country after forty-five years, and memories came flooding back. Uganda was her home. She loved the country where she had spent all her childhood. Visiting all the landmark structures brought back the memories of the past, and she wished she still lived in the most beautiful country in the world! A visit highly recommended.

Fatema's life in the UK and the harsh reality of her divorce from a sociopath, money-hungry 'husband' Shiraz are significant to her life. Her ex-husband ruined her son's career and tried everything to get the money and the house that he never paid for. This came as a blow to her, but Fatema turned it into her strength. This autobiographical book is one of the many examples of the iron will.

Chapter 1

It is ironic that Fatema's story begins with her exile from her beloved homeland. There would be no inspiration to write about her journey as an Asian in an African country had she not been viciously snatched away from the place she was born in. Fatema was born in Fort Portal, Uganda, and she was visiting her country after forty-five long years. Uganda was her home, where she had spent all her childhood. This was the place where all her happiest and her saddest memories were also born. The first time Fatema had given birth to her darling child, and the first time she realised that there was no place for people like her in this country anymore. The anguish she felt that day still wreaks havoc in her bones when she recalls abandoning her home country.

Fatema's son Arif wanted to visit Uganda to see the beautiful country his mum was born in. Mum had talked about the high standard of the education system and life in Uganda. She reluctantly agreed to go with him thinking of the politically unstable country she had left on 1 November 1972, forty-five years ago, when all Asians were expelled from Uganda. The ethnic cleansing of Asians in an African country is not something you hear about every day, yet it happened to them. Thousands of Asians were driven out of their homes, their bank accounts were frozen, their businesses and houses left behind were taken by so called

1

politicians and leaders. They were driven out of the country as mass exodus. African raiders were looting and mugging Asians' homes and businesses for their own material gains. There was a curfew, and army soldiers with guns occupied the country's streets. At times Fatema felt like she was witnessing a World War, yet the rest of the world was not affected in the least. Soldiers were everywhere in the capital city Kampala where she lived with her husband and his extended family. Her vivid memory of the chaotic country she had fled from with her ten-month-old baby daughter Amana, was petrifying. The thought of carrying a precious bundle that her child was while trying to stay alive is a memory that still brings her to tears of terror and anxiety.

Uganda had been a peaceful monarchy. Sure, it had its problems, but it never came close to cleaning out an entire race of people. Idi Amin was the chief commander of his army, who in January 1971, overthrew the government in a sudden violent, illegal seizure of power and took over the country. His new laws left him in complete power and control over the public. His tyranny lasted longer than most of them had hoped for, and the damage he caused cemented itself in the history as well as the minds of its people.

He was head of the state, and on 10 August, he declared that all Asians leave the country within three months, giving an ultimatum to depart by 10 November 1972. That had been a terrifying ordeal for Fatema and her family. They were forced out of their country, where they had spent their whole lives, and now, they needed to find new homes. They were airlifted to different countries.

Now in February 2018, she was returning to Uganda after almost half a century later. Fatema checked online the country's crime rate, the weather, and the cost of travelling to Uganda. She also contacted people she knew who had returned to Uganda and were living and running businesses there. She had a few of their phone numbers, so she contacted them; they reassured her regarding the country's safety and political stability. They advised her to hire a taxi which was the only mode of transportation for visitors and recommended her a hotel to stay in for a few nights. She checked online the availability of public transport, trains to different parts of the country, mainly to Fort Portal, west of Uganda; but the friends advised her that public transport was unreliable and would take days to get to and from places. She did not ever imagine going back to Uganda, as the bad memories of an unstable and disturbed country were distressing.

Further online search provided with more information about Uganda's past political history since its independence from the British Empire. The president appointed, Apollo Milton Obote, was a Ugandan political leader who led

Uganda to independence in October 1962. Under his administration, Uganda became the First Republic. She remembers it was rumoured at the time that Obote was planning to nationalise industries owned by Asians who were very wealthy and owned successful businesses and industries. She was a student at the time and did not take much interest in politics. To her innocent and ignorant mind, the country at the time seemed politically stable.

From Uganda's independence from Great Britain in 1962 to early 1971, Milton Obote's regime had terrorised, harassed, and tortured people. Obote's persecution of Indian traders was cruel barbaric. People were brutally exploited in the country as the government took over 60% share in major private corporations and banks in the country. There was flagrant and widespread corruption that emerged in the name of his version of "socialism". There was food shortage as Obote's persecution of Asian traders contributed to an excessive rise in prices of food and of all goods. The regime was disliked, particularly in Buganda, where people had suffered the most.

Obote faced a possible removal from office by factional infighting within his own party. He had four leading members of his party arrested and detained. He then suspended the federal constitution; and declared himself President of Uganda in February 1966, deposing Kabaka

Mutesa, (King Fredrick Mutesa) of Buganda. Obote wanted to remove all five monarchies of Uganda's Kingdoms that was over 1,000 years old, the oldest in East Africa. His hunger for power knew no bounds as he went on to destroy human lives and the country's economy for his personal gain.

The Buganda regional Parliament passed a resolution in May 1966 declaring that Buganda's incorporation into Uganda had legally ended with the suspension of the constitution and requesting the federal government (Obote's Gov) to vacate the capital city Kampala which was in the Buganda region. Obote responded with an armed attack upon the Kabaka's (King's) palace, sending Kabaka Mutesa into exile in the United Kingdom via Burundi, and in 1967 a new constitution abolished all of Uganda's kingdoms, including Buganda.

While in exile, Mutesa wrote an autobiography, 'The Desecration of My Kingdom'.

Sir Edward Frederick William David Walugembe Luwangula Mutesa II KBE (19 November 1924 – 21 November 1969) was Kabaka of the Kingdom of Buganda in Uganda from 22 November 1939. He took hold of the office at the tender age of 15, where he reigned under a Council of Regents, until he came of age and assumed full powers. He was the thirty-fifth Kabaka of Buganda and the first President of Uganda.

Mutesa died of alcohol poisoning in his London flat in 1969. Identified by the Metropolitan Police as suicide, the death has been viewed as assassination by those who claim Mutesa may have been force-fed vodka by agents of the Obote regime. Mutesa was interviewed in his flat only a few hours before his death by the British journalist who found that he was sober and in good spirits. He reported this to the police the following day on hearing of Mutesa's death, but the inquiry was not pursued. It seemed that the system had rotten to its core, and no one dared bat an eyelash at the murder of a supreme.

Mutesa's body was embalmed and returned to Uganda in 1971 after the overthrow of Obote and given a state funeral. The president who ordered the state funeral was Idi Amin, who at the time was army commander, had led the assault on Mutesa's palace in 1966. King Mutesa is buried in the Kasubi Tomb; kings of the Buganda dynasty are buried in Kasubi Mausoleum.

The Second Republic of Uganda existed from 1971 to 1979, when Uganda was ruled by Idi Amin's military dictatorship. Uganda's economy was destroyed by Amin's policies of nationalisation of businesses and industries and expansion of the public sector, including expulsion of

Asians, which resulted in a collapse of the economy by **90%** in less than a decade. The Ugandan politicians, the army generals who took over businesses and industries left behind by Asians, were not capable of running the businesses, the factories and industries, which was the major cause of the economic collapse.

The number of people killed as a result of Amin's regime is unknown; estimates from international observers and human rights groups range from 100,000 to 500,000.

Obote returned to Uganda in May 1980 after nine years in exile in Tanzania. He was re-elected on 17 December 1980, a year after Amin's overthrow in 1979. Obote's second period of rule ended in 1985 after a long and bloody conflict known as the Ugandan Bush War, also known as the Luwero, the Ugandan Civil War or the Resistance War. It was fought in Uganda by the official Ugandan government and its armed wing, the Uganda National Liberation Army (UNLA), against several rebel groups, most importantly the National Resistance Army (NRA). Amin was forced to flee the Ugandan capital by helicopter on 11 April 1979, when Kampala was captured. After a short-lived attempt to rally some remnants of the Uganda Army in eastern Uganda, which reportedly included Amin proclaiming the city of Jinja, his country's new capital, he fled into exile to Libya, where he stayed until 1980, and ultimately settled in Saudi Arabia.

After his second removal from power, Obote fled to Kenya and later to Zambia. In September 2005, it was reported that Obote would return to Uganda before the end of the year, but on 10 October 2005, Obote died of kidney failure in a hospital in Johannesburg, South Africa.

Yoweri Museveni (born 15 September 1944) is a Ugandan politician who has served as President of Uganda since 1986. Museveni was involved in rebellions that toppled Ugandan leaders Idi Amin (1971–79) and Milton Obote (1980–85) before he captured power and is the current president of Uganda, he has been in power since 1986. The country is safe and politically stable under Museveni rule. While it may take several years to bring back the similar prosperity and economic progress to the country that had flourished in Uganda prior to power-hungry leaders, Uganda has seen happier days under the leadership of Yoweri Museveni. With the help of the US Government, Museveni encouraged the exiled Asians to return and resume their businesses, offering residence permits, granting import licenses to businesses, and generally opening up the market for importation. Asian businesspeople started to return to their homeland to resume their own businesses and industries to repatriate capital and investments back to Uganda's economy.

Now, despite making up **less than 1%** of Uganda's population, Asians are estimated to contribute up to **65%** of Uganda's tax revenues.

Since their return to the country in the 1980s and 1990s, Asians from the Indian subcontinent have once again become **a pillar of the country's economy**. This economic prosperity had been snatched away from the people of Uganda based on Amin's mere personal bigotry and racism.

When Fatema and Arif called Raheem who had returned to Uganda he informed them that Uganda's President Musaveni visited the exiled wealthy Asians in person; he visited M Madhvani S Ruparelia, and many others, offering them help to resume their businesses.

The Asians returned to Uganda to rebuild their shattered businesses all over again. The Sugarcane Plantation, the Tea Plantation, the factories, and the industries that the Ugandans could not manage due to lack of experience were destroyed completely are now flourishing once again. The repatriated Asians helped Uganda back to its feet.

From running banks to farms to supermarkets to shopping malls, Ugandan Asians have regained their prominent role in the country's economy, following their mass expulsion decades ago.

J Sangram still remembers that fateful winter of 1972 when he, along with thousands of other Asians, was brutally hounded out of his home in Uganda by the almost psychopathic Idi Amin and forced to take refuge in an unwelcoming Britain.

Fatema felt at ease now that it was safe for both her and her son Arif to travel to Uganda. Arif bought a book titled 'Uganda' written by a lecturer/friend from his university who told him that he had returned to Fort Portal, Uganda. He is now retired, writes books in his leisure and travels to East Africa at times. He assured them that it was safe to travel to Uganda. Times had changed and there was lesser hate and intolerance, at least openly.

Arif booked the plane tickets online. They both had their travel injections, readied their visas and documents and soon flew from Birmingham Airport in Turkish Airline, that Fatema thought was the best airline ever, and she highly recommends it.

They arrived in Istanbul at 10 am. There was a twenty-four-hour stopover in Istanbul, where their luggage transferred over to the next flight to Uganda. They both had their hand luggage with them, for a night stopover. From the machines at Ataturk Airport, Istanbul Arif purchased entry visas and exchanged Turkish currency called Lira. He bought the Metro day-passes from the machine, and they went sightseeing. Istanbul is a beautiful city with attractive architecture that is famous all over the world for its classic designs. The weather in Istanbul is similar to UK's weather, cold but sunny on a February morning. They visited the beautiful Blue Mosque, a striking, iconic building built in 1616 by Sultan Ahmed. It is a principal mosque in Istanbul; there is also a handwritten copy of the Quran by Hazarat Usman, one of the rulers of the faith. Both of them performed afternoon prayers in the mosque, which felt like a divine experience in itself. They also visited the nearby Sophia Hagia Museum, which was once a church and was converted into a mosque by the Ottoman Empire in 1453, after the fall of Constantinople. Later on, they had a meal at a nearby restaurant; and stayed in a bed and breakfast that Arif had pre-booked prior to flying there. She had been thinking about her return to Uganda. It had been so long that all memories of her homeland were blurry and distant to her. She wondered if she will feel nostalgic. Fatema's main aim of travelling to different countries was to tinder a partnership for her son. She was hoping he would find his match.

The next morning after breakfast, they got a taxi back to Ataturk Airport. The flight time was 10 am to Entebbe International Airport, Uganda; on the plane, they were given hot meals which helped them sleep comfortably later. The plane arrived in Uganda at 5 am the next morning. The weather in the early hours of the morning was hot and humid. They took a taxi from Entebbe Airport, and instructed the driver about where they wanted to go. It had been years for her, too, so they decided they will have a small tour in the taxi first, mainly to accustom themselves to the weather that was all too familiar yet alien to them. The taxi driver took them around Entebbe city and then to the warm sandy beach of Lake Victoria. He told them the lake was right outside, just a few meters from the departure gate of Entebbe Airport.

The roads were clear in the early hours of the day. It was an hour's drive to Kampala, the capital city of Uganda. The driver, as instructed, took them to Lubiri, the Kabaka's palace at Mengo, Kampala, where they merely got an outside view of the palace, because the entry is prohibited.

Ronald Edward Frederick Kimera Muwenda Mutebi II (born 13 April 1955) is the reigning Kabaka (king) of the Kingdom of Buganda, a constitutional kingdom in modern-day Uganda. He is the 36th Kabaka of Buganda. Thanks to Idi Amin for restoring the monarchies, which was the desire of Buganda Tribe, the largest in the country, making it considerably influential too.

They visited Idi Amin's dungeon, where many of Amin's opponents were electrocuted. Amin was known as a "Butcher of Uganda" for the ruthlessness and brutality of his regime. Corruption ran rampant during his time in power. It is said more than 500,000 people were murdered under his rule, not to mention the brutal ethnic cleansing, political suppression, extrajudicial murders, and other human rights violations.

They also saw Gaddafi Mosque, which is a beautiful landmark with a stunning structure. It is open to public and is located in the Old Kampala area. Completed in 2006, it seats up to 15,000 worshipers and can hold another 1,100 in the gallery, while the terrace will cater for another 3,500.

Colonel Muammar Gaddafi of Libya commissioned the mosque as a gift to Uganda, and for the benefit of the Muslim population. Uganda has many mosques, but Gaddafi is the first skyscraper mosque of Uganda.

The two of them then also visited the graveyard where Arif's paternal great grandfather is buried and offered a prayer on their ancestors' and other relatives' graves. They also visited Old Kampala, where Fatema and her husband's extended family used to live, and where the primary school was located where she used to work as a teacher. The city

Kampala has dense traffic and high population, the driver had to navigate to all these sights with careful planning because of the uncertainty in the routes. Then finally, they got to the hotel Crown Jakiba that she had pre-booked online; the hotel is located directly opposite their mosque. They had their meals and went to the mosque for Thursday evening prayers and service. There they met with other friends who had returned to Kampala and were happily settled back into the country. They met a 94-year-old 'Uncle' Ibrahim who was Fatema's father's friend, who, to her utter astonishment, looked very fit and drove his own car. His daughter Mubina was a student in the same Teacher's Training College as Fatema. They also met Rahman, an old family friend.

The next afternoon they attended Friday prayers at the mosque and gave tins of chocolates to Uncle Ibrahim and to Rahman, who both invited her and Arif for a meal at a private beach of Lake Victoria. Due to a shortage of time, they could not accept their invitations. She regrettably declined their invitations. Their earlier adventures had been on the way to their hotel in Kampala and Fatema was feeling jetlagged from the journey. The intense city heat and the anxiety of coming back to a country that once exiled her had also been fresh in her mind, but now she had settled a little and put her mind at ease. She decided she was ready to enjoy the sweet nostalgic smell of her old Uganda. Arif wanted to visit all the famous sights and landmarks of the country.

After a night in the hotel, they arranged with Jeffrey, the taxi driver, to take them sightseeing to other parts of the country. Arif wanted to visit all the famous sights and landmarks of the country. She revisited all the main popular landmarks that she had visited with her parents and siblings as a child a long time ago. This tour was the most enjoyable experience of a lifetime for both her and her son, whom she did not see connecting with her homeland the way she had.

Uganda is a landlocked country in East Africa and is bordered by Kenya in the east, Sudan in the north, to the west, The Republic of Congo and to the south by Tanzania.

English has been Uganda's lone official language since independence in **1962**. In 2005 Swahili, which is foreign and so viewed as being neutral, was proposed as the country's second official language. But this has yet to be ratified by parliament.
4 Nov 2015

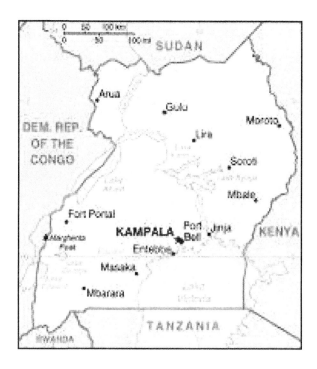

The southern part of the country includes a substantial portion of Lake Victoria, shared with Kenya and Tanzania. Uganda is in the African Great Lakes region. Uganda also lies within the Nile basin and has a varied but a generally modified equatorial climate.

At the beginning of 1894, the country was ruled as a protectorate by the United Kingdom, which established administrative law across the territory. The country's first elected president, Apollo Milton Obote (born 28 December 1925 – 10 October 2005) was Uganda's first political leader who led Uganda to independence from British colonial rule. Uganda gained independence from the UK on 9 October 1962 with Queen Elizabeth II as head of state and Queen of

Uganda. In October 1963, Uganda became a republic but maintained its membership in the Commonwealth Nations.

The coat of arms of Uganda was adopted three weeks before declaring independence by the Uganda Legislative Council. On 1 October 1962, the arms were approved by Governor of Uganda Walter Coutts, and formally established by law on 9 October 1962.

Motto is: For God and My Country

The shield and spears represent the willingness of the Ugandan people to defend their country. The Kob (antelope) represents abundant wildlife; the green represents the fertile land and the blue directly above is a representation of The Nile, the longest river in the world. The Crested Crane was chosen as Uganda's national emblem because of its beauty and elegance. It is a bird of national significance to Uganda, occupying a prime position on the country's national flag and coat of arms. The Crested Crane has been Uganda's symbol for nearly 100 years.

The three colours of the Uganda flag are representative of Native ethnic groups of Africa (black), Africa's sunshine (yellow), and African brotherhood (red being the colour of blood, through which all Africans are connected).

Chapter 2

Uganda is the most beautiful country in the world. It is called the Pearl of Africa, a piece of heaven on earth. Its beauty is exemplary even though the country has seen more than its fair share of massacres and destruction. With a booming economy, mild weather, and breath-taking landscapes, flora, and fauna. There is no doubt as to why Winston Churchill referred to it as the "Pearl of Africa."

The main attraction is the Murchison Falls National Park that has recorded the largest number of visitors when 104,000 tourists visited in the year 2018 to 2019.

Early Saturday morning, the pre-arranged taxi driver, Jeffrey, with Fatema and Arif, travelled to Murchison Falls National Park. The roads were good, and the vision was clear. Fatema was surprised to see the vast improvement in the condition of the roads.

She remembered when she was a young girl, Uganda had narrow Murram roads that are now much wider and beautiful Tarmac Highways. This surprise brought a smile of approval to her face. The weather was hot and humid in the morning, temperature 27°C. This she clearly remembered, the perspiring heat of the city where they would have to survive throughout the day. After a long drive, they arrived at their destination. They bought tickets for the entrance to the game park. The ferry took them across the River Nile to the park to see the game reserve, where they watched animals in their natural habitat. At the riverbanks, they saw elephants drinking water and bathing, trying to cool themselves down from the midday heat temperature of 31°C. It was a pleasant view. The sight of looking at so many living beings made Fatema feel more alive and grateful for the life she had.

Safari drives are a very enjoyable experience here. You can see abundance of wildlife in their natural habitat. The twittering and roaring of the animals chorusing in their perfect symphony. The ranger/guide knows and understands the location of animals and where the animals and birds are found. He also knows the names of the birds like Bushbucks, Shoebill, and Crested Crane etc.

Fatema was indeed feeling a lot better that she had come to Uganda after years. She felt safe, more at home. She remembers when she was a little girl, she had visited the park with her parents and siblings. She was grateful to her son for convincing her to visit Uganda, her homeland that she could not forget.

The vehicle in which one is travelling crosses the river by ferry to the Safari Park. The ferry takes you to the other side of the river, where the Ranger armed with a gun sits in the taxi in the passenger's seat. He instructs the driver to drive through the narrow murram roads and through the routes that leads to exotic African wildlife, where they can be seen resting under trees and bushes sheltering from the sun and heat. The Ranger instructed the driver to slow down when animals were sighted. They went close and stopped, switched off the engine, so the animals would not be disturbed when they took close-up videos and photos. They all looked so majestic, soaking in the sun and looking like they ruled the lands. Fatema was in awe of their beauty.

With the help of the expert guide, they managed to see lots of deer, kobs, elephants, buffalos, hippos, giraffes, and lions that, according to the Ranger, are rare to see. Some buffalos were at the lakeside, the guide informed them the lake was called Lake Albert with its beautiful soft sandy beach. They took lots of photos and videos. Going around the park is a very educational and exciting experience. They could see all the animals in their actual size. The African elephants are the world's largest land mammals, are larger than Asian elephants. The huge elephants are herbivore, feed on plants only, drink 210 litres of water and spend 16 hours foraging every day.

Giraffes, a head above the rest, the world's tallest land mammals, are also herbivore; their long necks and long legs help them get leaves and twigs of tall Acacia trees, their favourite food. Fatema watched the giraffes run really fast around the park. They looked amazing with their long necks nodding with them. The guide told them when chased by predators like lions, the giraffe can run up to 55 km/h.

Uganda is gifted with a variety of physical features and is blessed with all kinds of wildlife with beautiful landscape. A four-hour guided tour round the game park enables one to see abundant wildlife, followed by a visit to the top of the falls. The park's main feature is the world's longest river 6,695 km, The Victoria Nile, which is the source of the Murchison Falls. The most spectacular sight, exclusively scenic in itself.

The entire Nile that is 50 meters wide forces itself through a gorge measuring 7 meters wide. The thunderous noise made by the force of water as it passes through tiny space and drops down 43 meters is magnificent. It is the most beautiful and the most powerful waterfall in the world; a true masterpiece, not to be missed.

Fatema remembers a long time ago, she had risked going across a rope bridge when she visited the falls with her parents and siblings. The driver explained that due to the force of the river the bridge was washed away, and now there are metal barriers for protection.

After the safari, there was a boat cruise, the maid of the mist – which is an option; the boat takes one up the river Victoria Nile to the trail leading to the base of the Murchison Falls. You are given waterproof hooded jackets, but you would still get soaked with the cool mist of water spray from the falls that feels pleasant on your arms and face in the midday heat. Natural phenomenon: a waterfall turns into a beautiful fountain of colours to form a rainbow as sunlight reflects off its wet spray. Arif couldn't believe how lucky he was to see such a sight, and just had to start taking pictures.

The return journey back on the ferry across the river, and Jeffrey's taxi took them to the top of the falls, which was the best part of the trip, for all it was a most breathtaking spectacular sight!

Due to high demand, pre-booking in advance is recommended for bed and breakfast at Nile Safari Lodge or at Kabalega Lodge. For food and accommodation, Fatema and Arif decided to go to Masindi, a town nearby.

The town near Murchison Falls is Fort Portal, which by car is 1 hour and 10 min; to Masindi is 1 hour 30 min where food, bed and breakfast are available at comparative prices.

Fatema, Arif and Jeffrey had a meal and stayed at a Bed and Breakfast in Masindi. The next day, they continued their journey towards Fort Portal to visit Fatema's childhood home where she lived with her parents and siblings; and also see the Hot Springs in Bundibugyo, Wamba. The journey took a whole day as they stopped in a town called Hoima, where Jeffrey's mother lived with her adult children and her grandchildren in a big five-bedroom house. She gave them some bananas; they bought some bottled water and food from a shop to eat on the journey. They passed through a lot of villages, namely Kenjojo and Butiti, and finally arrived in Fort Portal, passing the tea plantations near the ranges of Mount Rwenzori. From distance, they observed the tea plantation that looked like a green carpet dotted with large trees and tea pickers with baskets attached to their backs. The greenery surrounding the village was a refreshing sight!

Fatema had happy memories of Fort Portal, where she had spent all her childhood. The weather is cooler in the West of Uganda; she remembered it to be unpolluted and the most beautiful place in the world.

They passed the beautiful structure that is the Royal Palace of the Omukama (King) of Toro Kingdom is found on Kabarole Hill near the serene Fort Portal, on the opposite side is Fatema's school, St Anne's Junior Secondary School. They stopped at the graveyard to pay their respect and offer prayers on Fatema's brother's grave and other graves of many relatives who are buried there. *"Peace be upon you all, O inhabitants of the dwellings (i.e. the graves), amongst the believers..."* it is recommended visiting graveyard for two reasons: one, it reminds them of death and two, they can pray for the people buried there.

They visited Fatema's 'home', which had now become government offices and shops; Fatema couldn't even recognise the place. The town had grown twenty times more and was overpopulated. All the Asian businesses are now occupied by black Ugandans who are friendly and welcoming. Fatema and Arif learned that they wanted all Asians to 'return' to Uganda.

It was late in the evening, they could hear calls for Muslim prayers. Jeffrey said there were several mosques all in the same village. Fatema explained the different sects of

Islam being Shia, Sunni, Bohra and others. Just like Christianity have Catholic and Protestants who all go to different churches.

They booked a Bed and Breakfast on Wamba Road and went to a nearby restaurant for a delicious meal of Ugandan local staple diet Matoke (green bananas), Mogo (cassava), pumpkin and meat.

The next morning, they travelled to Wamba to see The Hot Springs.

The Sempaya Hot Springs in Uganda form one of the natural attractions. Boiling hot water, naturally occurring, produced by the emergence of geothermal-heated groundwater from the earth's crust is formed when water meets the heated hot rocks.

The heated water is forced back up under pressure to bubble as a hot spring. The water in the springs can warm up to 120 °C (248 °F), and temperature of the hot springs can boil an egg in 10 minutes. Hot springs are traditionally believed to be having healing powers. Most local communities around the hot springs believe that it has the divine powers and performs miracles and is worshipped by local people who believe the gods reside in the hot springs. Scientifically, the water from the hot springs has been found to contain varying amounts of minerals and chemicals that are known to have medicinal values in them.

It is estimated that about 800 people visit some of the springs per week to bathe. When bathing in a hot spring, the dense clouds of steam rise above the rippling water to bathe you in beads of moisture. This is equivalent to being in a sauna, fully clothed. Visitors boil eggs, potatoes, and green bananas (matoke) and eat lunch cooked in the hot springs. Fatema's group and the guide had their hot, freshly cooked lunch there, in a sheltered place with tables and benches for tourists. It was an intense day with mid-day heat temperature rising to 32 °C.

The guide took them to the other side of the hot spring, called the 'male hot spring' where water was slightly cooler. He managed to fill two bottles of water for Fatema to take and use it for her bath as it has healing powers.

They had a guided tour to see the local wildlife such as monkeys, chimpanzees, exotic birds and snakes all on the tall palm trees. The guide explained about the local people, the Pygmies, who regularly visit the hot springs to perform their rituals.

The Pygmy Village nearby is one of the tourist attractions.

The Pygmies are the shortest people ever seen. A full adult male is no more than five feet tall; they are under serious threat of going extinct. This population is rapidly decreasing as deforestation, poverty, intermarriage with Bantu peoples and Westernisation are gradually destroying their way of life and culture. The Pygmies are a group of hunter-gatherers, and while there are still 250,000 of them still remaining, they are quickly reducing in numbers. There might come a time when we will only read that there used to be a Pygmy tribe with the most unusual features and heights.

After these visits, they travelled back to Kampala, going back via Fort Portal and through Mubende district and to Crown Jakiba Hotel for one night. Fatema remembered as a child visiting her aunt who lived in Mubende town, then a small village that is now grown ten times more and is not recognisable. The small urban towns that were left behind by Asians in the 1970s are now developed and grown into large cities.

The next day they visited their final tourists' attraction, the Line of Equator at Mpigi near Entebbe. The return flight to Birmingham, UK, via Istanbul, was the same night from Entebbe International Airport.

The Line of Equator is a landmark in Uganda. The Equator is the only line of latitude which is a great circle.

Uganda is one of the few countries in the world where the imaginary Line of Equator passes through that divides the earth into two halves, that are the northern and the southern hemisphere. The Line crosses into Uganda at a point situated 75 km south of Kampala, along the Kampala – Masaka road. The equator is in Kayabwe, Mpigi District, approximately 72 kilometres from Kampala city if you are driving southwest of Kampala through the country near Entebbe where Fatema and Arif visited and took lots of videos and pictures and cemented a part of wonder in their memories.

It is known that the gravity is weaker at the equator due to forces produced by the planet earth's rotation acceleration at the poles is 980.665 cm/sec/sec while at the equator it is 3.39 cm/sec/sec less, due to the centrifugal force.

If you weighed 100 pounds at the North Pole, at the equator, you would weigh 99.65 pounds, or 5.5 ounces less.

Uganda enjoys equatorial weather, which is perfect all year round with temperatures between 16°C night/ -28°C day for most of the year. In general, temperatures are pleasant with warm or hot days and cooler nights. The dry season is experienced from December to February and June to July. Daylight hours are 12.1 hours all the year round. The rainy season from March till May and October to November.

It never rains but it pours in Kampala, Uganda; the water comes down in buckets for only a few minutes. The heavy shower passes as quickly as it comes, sun comes out again and dries the streets clean. It is a welcome relief, it cools the day, leaving the air smelling fresh.

The Line of Equator also passes through Kasese, near Fort Portal, the place known as Queen Elizabeth National Park; the landmark is a tourist attraction that also offers a three-day Safari lodge stay and tours to National Park to see the wildlife and enjoy the local food. Uganda's staple diet is green bananas, steam-cooked in banana leaves and mashed; served with steamed or boiled fish or meat or chicken. Fatema believes it to be the tastiest meal she has ever eaten, A Taste of Africa.

Mount Rwenzori National Park is located within the "Mountains of the Moon", as Mt Rwenzori it is called, is situated in Western Uganda.

The mountain is the third highest in Africa rising more than 16,700 feet above sea level and its highest peaks rise above the clouds and are permanently snow-capped. The Rwenzori Mountain Ranges are higher compared to the Alps, and they have glaciers that are one of the sources of the longest river on earth, The River Nile.

The Mt. Ruwenzori region is the most seismically active region in Uganda that influence the occurrence of earthquakes in the Toro district, West Uganda. The epicentre in Uganda recorded various earthquakes that occurred in the past. In 1966 earthquake had a magnitude of Mw 6.8:66.

Fatema's father told them to evacuate immediately; they all rushed outside on the street in their nightwear, the house was shaking, there were cracks, and homes were not inhabitable. The community centres like mosques and temples accommodated them until the houses were safe to return to. Fatema remembered despite the natural disaster that had occurred in her hometown, the community had come together to survive, and everyone was taking care of each other. She had felt warm and happy at the thought that humans were all united against a common threat. This memory reminded her of the terrible occurrences that had driven her and her family away from Uganda forty-five years ago. She could not help but marvel at the contrast in human nature.

The causes of earthquakes in Uganda are associated with rifting movements in the East African Rift System (EARS). The western border of Uganda lies in the western arm of EARS which is highly seismically active. Other faults are weak zones that influence the occurrence of earthquakes in Uganda. Various earthquakes that occurred in the past were recorded.

20 March 1966, the Rwenzori earthquake occurred in Toro district measured 6.6 on Richter scale. This earthquake killed 150 people and injured 1,300 people. It caused an economic loss estimated at US $1 million. Fatema has vivid memory of this earthquake that was preceded by numerous foreshocks and was followed by many aftershocks during the next two months, nine of them with a magnitude of 5.0 or greater. The fierce force of the earthquake shook their homes in the early hours of the morning. They were woken up by the rumbling noise and shaking of the house.

The Mt. Ruwenzori region is the most seismically active region in Uganda and also one of the most seismically active zones in the EARS and is bounded by steep active faults. The calculated focal mechanism for the earthquake was normal faulting in type, although the focal mechanisms of three of the aftershocks were dominantly strike-slip (movement between rocks) in type.

Ground shaking due to the movement of rocks in the mountain is the primary cause of earthquakes that damage man-made structures. Many factors influence the strength of earthquake shaking at a site, including the earthquake's magnitude, the site's proximity to the fault, the local geology, and the soil type.

The 1966 earthquake caused the educational institutions to remain closed across Toro district due to continuous tremors. The students at Asian Primary School in Fort Portal were attending classes under trees. The school headmaster had decided to hold classes under the trees in order to ensure that students were not deprived of education.

The schools' classrooms were unsafe to return to; most of the classes were conducted in open playgrounds, each teacher with their small class of children, under shelters of trees and temporary built Marquee tents. This was possible as most children stayed at home. The weather was fine all year round. The insurance companies assessed the damage and repair work took a few months. Fortunately, most dwellings, offices and schools were single-storey buildings that had suffered only minimal damage.

Fatema remembers she was in her late teens at the time and was on her teaching practice as she was an auxiliary teacher.

Thinking of those happy days of her childhood brought back happy memories; the Asians were happily settled, and Uganda was their home.

Chapter 3

For generations, many Asians from India and Pakistan had settled in Uganda and had British Passports. Because the country was politically unstable, most Asians held on to their British passports. By 19th and 20th century, there were over eighty-seven thousand Asians in Uganda. From running banks to farms to supermarkets to shopping malls, Ugandan Asians have gained an important and a main role in the country's economy. At the time, they owned **90%** of the country's businesses and accounted for **90%** of Ugandan tax revenues.

Although all Asians looked or dressed alike and have brown skin, but due to religious differences they did not mingle with each other as one community. Religion being the main aspect of life was the main reason for division. There were Hindus who congregated in their own temples called Mandir; the Sikhs went to their own Gurudwara; Muslims also had divisions: Shia Muslim, Sunni Muslims, Aghakhanis, Wahabis, Bohra, all went to their own places of worship. There was no unity among the people. They were all the same people and had the same culture but considered themselves to be superior to the other based on their minor changes in beliefs. Asians living in the same city/town had their own establishments. Asians did not mingle with Black Ugandans as they not only had different cultures but also had their own beliefs and churches. Religion, once again, was the main reason of division between the communities. Intermingling and intermarriages were discouraged or mostly forbidden in all communities and in all religions, so there was also no hope of unifying strength in the shape of a marital union.

It was end of World War II in the mid/late forties when Fatema was born in Fort Portal, West Uganda, the capital city of Toro kingdom. It is one of Uganda's most scenic districts located at the foot of ranges of The Rwenzori Mountain. Fatema had two older sisters, three younger sisters and three younger brothers, who all lived in a five bedroomed house. The house had two reception rooms, two guest rooms and a servants' quarters. Most houses were single-storey built with these facilities and traditionally almost everyone had large families and servants.

Fatema's father, Ali, owned a shop that sold fabric/material and other groceries. He employed two tailors and provided sewing machines to them who stitched clothes for customers who bought material from his shop. He also employed shop assistants and worked hard to provide for his family. Ali's wife Noor, Fatema's mother, also helped in the shop whenever she could when all the children were older and capable of caring for themselves without requiring constant attention.

Both Ali and Noor were religious and were well respected by their community. They arranged community gatherings in their own house for which two rooms were secluded for ladies and men separate, segregated for regular religious gatherings. For Thursday night prayers, services, ceremonies, Friday prayers and other religious rituals, Ali and Noor cooked food and served it at the community's religious rituals and services that were all held in his house. It was a bonding tradition that the two enjoyed. The Muslim community would come together at these festivals and events and become a part of each other's lives, in happiness and sadness. It was the true example of brotherhood. When the community increased and grew in numbers, they decided to rent a bigger hall to accommodate them all during services and ceremonies; until Ali and committee members of his mosque managed to raise funds to build a mosque. Funds were collected in various ways: from his own community members and Ali also travelled to all towns in Uganda, to the capital city Kampala where there were many wealthy donors. Ali's friend Ibrahim lived in Kampala, who was a generous donor; Ali also got a large amount of money from the World Federation of Muslim Communities. They collected enough funds to build the first mosque in their town. The building of their very first mosque was an enormous gesture on their part. They were becoming solid members of the community and had already made a name for themselves, a respectable name at that.

Ali also arranged many religious preachers/ministers from abroad, mainly from India. Urdu speaking preachers were summoned to deliver sermons and preach Islam to community members and to their children; Ali provided accommodation and welfare of the preachers in his own house. Each preacher had a three-year contract, after which a new preacher replaced him. It could be seen as giving a chance to priests from all over the lands and having them over so they could increase the knowledge of the community in their own various and singular ways.

Fatema remembered having religious discussions/talks and debates with the preachers. Fatema's father was a very caring person, told her that she would make a good lawyer but she, like all the children at her age, wanted to be a doctor.

Fatema's mother Noor always helped in the shop; both parents helped each other with the housework, both were good cooks. They did everything together, including cooking food for the community functions and rituals. Fatema lived in the house where she and her siblings were nuch loved by both parents. They were a happy family altogether. Everyone in the house had a good relationship with the other, and they helped each other out. There was no such thing as duties assigned to one which the other could not help with. Fatema grew up knowing loving to help her family and loved ones.

Everyone in the community gathered regularly for prayers and other ceremonies/rituals in the mosque; the community at large were close with each other and arranged social gatherings/activities and excursions/picnics together and travelled in a hired van. Fatema and all her siblings had a very contented life. Everyone spoke the Ugandan language Rutoro and Swahili that was commonly spoken with African workers.

Uncle Shaban, Ali's younger brother by two years, also lived in Fort Portal with his family of four daughters and three sons. He also had a shop. Ali cared for him and treated Shaban like his son rather than his brother. Uncle Shaban was a fun loving, a good hearted person, and his children, Fatema's cousins, had a close relationship with Fatema's family. All cousins were good friends and Uncle Shaban, like Fatema's father Ali, was the best person in the world in the eyes of the kids. He was a very caring person and took all children to the cinema, theatres, circus, playground, amusement parks, and funfairs. Fatema knows Uncle Shaban loved his brother's children more than his own. Aunty Rubab, his wife, frequently reminded him that his duty to his own children comes first. Aunty Rubab's brother Tahir was close to his sister's children. He bought presents for his nieces and nephews. All in all, Fatema's immediate and extended family were all connected to each other and loved spending time together. Fatema had indeed grown up in an environment where she felt safe and comforted by her parents, siblings, and relatives.

In the era where there were no restrictions on women's clothing, girls wore school uniforms, miniskirts, PE shorts and there was no hair covering for women. Men and women of the community mingled with each other and went on picnics together. In some Indian cultures, once women were married, they were expected to cover their legs and wear traditional Asian clothes.

Everyone had two or more black Ugandan servants to do the house chores and look after children. Most Asians who were shopkeepers also had shop assistants and drivers to transport rolls of material and other goods from factories/warehouses to shops. It was a proper and fair arrangement for all parties involved and helped work more in lesser time.

Fatema's eldest sister Banu became extremely ill when she was one. She had a high temperature that resulted in hearing impairment which also affected her speech. As a baby, Banu was a very beautiful bonny baby. Pictures/photos show all Noor's and Ali's children were beautiful, chubby, healthy and well. After completing her primary education,

Banu stayed at home where she learnt to cook and sew clothes. Sukyna, the second sister, was ill during exams and did not pass entrance exams to JS (Junior Secondary) so she had to repeat it twice, which resulted in her falling behind the third daughter, Fatema, in education. Rukaya, the fourth daughter, went to Mbarara boarding school and thereafter to Mulago Nursing Hospital for nursing qualification. Ali and Noor made sure to educate their children, especially daughters, because they knew it was crucial to be independent.

Uganda's official language is English. The education system in all schools and the medium of instruction is English. All Fatema's siblings went to the private Asian Primary school where they also learnt to read and write Gujrati, an Asian language that was spoken widely among all Asians. The other languages that most Asians spoke was Hindi, Urdu, Sindh, and African languages, Swahili and Rutoro which are mainly spoken by the West Ugandan tribe. One good thing about the Ugandan culture that Fatema admired the most was its diverse culture; people came from different walks of life with different cultures and traditions. They spoke many languages, yet there was always a feeling of association.

Every day after school Fatema, her siblings and all Muslim children went to learn to read Arabic Quran at a lady's house; and thereafter went home for tea and played badminton with next-door adult friends in the back garden, where they also played card games, Ludo etc. in the evening before dinner. There was an air of friendliness and positivity in the community where everyone knew everyone and came together to have fun times with each other. It is a rare thing to witness these days in the era of mobile phones and private lives.

Fatema's parents prepared to go to a Holy Pilgrimage to Hajj in Mecca and Madinah, and to all the holy cities in Saudi Arabia to perform Islamic rituals; leaving Aunty Faiza, Fatema's maternal aunt who was in her fifties, to look after the family and Aunty Faiza's 25-year-old son, Cousin Amar who was unemployed, was to look after the shop that Father Ali owned. They came a week in advance prior to Fatema's parents' departure to get trained and understand how everything worked and get used to the children's routine. There were servants and maids that did the house chores and shop assistants to help with the shop, but they all also needed guidance from a supervisor, a role that was temporarily being given to Aunty Faiza and her son Amar. In the absence of the parents, Cousin Amar played cards games and gambling games with friends and neighbours at night-time and slept in the daytime, leaving shop assistants to manage the shop.

Whilst the parents were away, Fatema's two-year-old second brother Yasar became extremely ill. He had a high temperature and had an epileptic fit that resulted in loss of hearing and affected his speech. As a young baby, Yasar was frequently ill and was crying a lot. The family doctor advised that he may have lactose intolerance or milk protein allergy, a rare genetic condition, so he should feed him on plant-based milk alternative Horlicks. Yasar was fed on Horlicks before the parents went for Hajj, but Aunty Faiza may have overlooked this and may have run out of stock and started giving him regular milk that he cannot digest, resulting in him getting seriously sick. Aunty Faiza and Cousin Amar were worried, they contacted the mosque preacher who looked in the holy book, The Quran and advised them to change his name to Mohsar, as Yasar was a 'weighty' name, and it was a name of the chapter from the Holy Book. His name did not change.

After 4 months, the parents returned from the Hajj journey; they had a shock! The shop was empty and all the goods, materials, rolls of textile, and all other goods in the shop were gone; the shop was in deficit. Cousin Amar was negligent in his duty; the loss of income subsequently resulted in a financial shortfall. Ali was devastated. He had to borrow from a company, The Bhimani's Department Stores, who were wealthy shop owners from his own community and restart the business all over again. It was with great difficulty that he could rebuild his business; he had a family of nine children to feed. It took a long time to rebuild his business. The family suffered, too, because their running business was suddenly now seeing losses due to negligence from a family member, and now they had to pick up the broken pieces of their fortune by themselves, as no one was there to help them out.

 In the days when there was no electricity, in small villages; streets and homes were lit up with kerosene lanterns. Ali was in the shop working until late one evening using kerosene lanterns, when suddenly he was engulfed with smoke. The plastic bags hanging above the lantern melted, causing a fire. Ali was saved but the shop was completely burnt down; all documents, children's birth certificates, passports, his brother Shaban's documents, everything lost in ashes. Once again, he was devastated! He would have to start all over again.

Ali and Noor, his wife, decided to move to a small village, in Bundibugyo near Fort Portal and start a new shop all over again. He had to sell his property, his home to The Bhimani's and start with a small shop in Bundibugyo. He had to rent his own home in Fort Portal to educate his children in government-funded schools and colleges. It was a terrible ordeal for Fatema's family. They had suffered another huge blow after the family was already in shambles, and now to start anew would take lots of hard work and courage. They were in a state where all members of the family needed to pitch in and save the family business.

Ali's brother, Shaban, sold his shop and also moved to be near Ali. Both brothers were close to each other now, both emotionally and physically, and decided to help each other out in these trying times. Both brothers set up their shops in Bundibugyo village. At the time there was no electricity in the small village. Some houses had tap water and water tanks that filtered rainwater collected in tanks. Everyone had kerosene stoves and clay cookers/ovens in the kitchen. They cooked on the clay ovens and kerosene stoves and heated water for a bath on the clay cookers that were heated with wood or charcoal. Some had gas cylinders attached to gas cookers, more like camping stoves. It was like Fatema had travelled back in time and was now experiencing things backwards. She had seen luxury previously, but now her family's wealth had deteriorated. She needed to start over and help her family get back on their feet. They had to transfer from a city to a village where they could not properly get the basic necessities. Fatema remembered that time to be incredibly difficult for her family.

47

Ali and his brother both were selling material, clothes and other goods. They were settling there when one night, Uncle Shaban's shop caught fire. Still, fortunately, they managed to extinguish it with water, with minimal damage.

During school holidays, the family went to Bundibugyo to spend holidays with Father Ali. Bundibugyo is a small village, located near the hot springs; they always stopped at the hot springs, cooked food, and had picnics.

There was a family next door to Ali's shop, Uncle Yusuf and Aunty Zahra, their older daughter Rubab, who was the same age as Fatema, came over and they played card games together. Their younger brother Malik was about eighteen, very tall and attractive, told Fatema that he was going to marry her. Fatema, 22 took no notice of him as he was too young.

Galeb, the most beautiful baby, was the youngest member of Fatema's family; had an accident when he was a year old. He fell from the top window of a double-storey house onto the concrete staircase bellow, headfirst! He was rushed to the hospital, where he had an emergency operation. The young doctor who operated on him explained that two rods were placed in his soft baby skull to lift it in order to save the brain that was fortunately intact. While Galeb was in the Intensive Care Unit, the whole family prayed for him. The family had a strong faith in prayers and relied upon it.

The next morning miraculously, he woke up safe. He recovered, but he had a slight hearing impairment as he grew older because he had suffered a traumatic head injury at a very tender age.

Fatema's brother Suleiman, five years younger to her but eldest of the three boys, when coming home from school, was pushed by his cousin on the road. A truck ran him over and he was instantly killed. It was the most tragic incident that shook the whole village, especially his parents and family – a boy child born after five daughters, handsome, six-foot-tall, who died in his early teens only fourteen. His sudden death was a deep loss and a real tragedy to his family and parents, especially his father.

The whole village was in shock. They all sympathised with Ali and his unfortunate family. Ali never got over it. He sobbed for the rest of his life. Fatema knows her father was the most caring person in the world. His unconditional love for his children was overwhelming. The tragic death of such a young person was the most difficult thing to accept or to overcome. Ali aged suddenly because of the grief, his hair turned grey, his face wrinkled, and he looked old. All his friends, his community members could not recognise him; they comforted him by offering help with the shop, but he could not be consoled. Ali was saying, 'When Prophet Jacob's son Joseph was taken away from him, he knew his son was alive, but he cried for a long time; my son is never coming back!'

Five days later, Fatema's mother Noor opened the shop and tried to continue with the business. Gradually Ali joined her to help and eventually, with great difficulty, started the business again.

Their life had been incredibly tragic and unfortunate, their business got closed twice, and their children got hurt. One even died. Yet, Fatema's family held tight together and persevered. It was a devastating time for everyone, but they stayed strong for each other.

Chapter 4

Fort Portal was a tiny town, so the only Asian school was the private primary school. After five years in the private school education at the age of ten, students had to pass 11+ exams to be admitted into Junior/Secondary schools. Most children went to Kampala, the capital city, for further studies in Asian Junior/Secondary Schools. Fatema's father's shop had a financial deficit and had debts; therefore, Fatema went to a government-funded, all girls' African school, St Anne's Junior/Secondary Catholic school. After that, she went to all girls Kinyamasika Teachers Training College (TTC) in Fort Portal. Where there were only three Asians girls. The rest were all black African girls in both establishments. Fatema felt a little out of place, but she soon got used to it, being a minority Asian in a majority Black community. She got along well with each other but would have felt a little more comfortable with more Asians/Muslims around who understood her culture and upbringing.

Fatema recalls her life at St Anne's JS as being the best in her life. She wore a school uniform of red short, pleated skirt, white blouse with a short red tie, white socks, and black shoes. Her best friend Florence Lily was an attractive black girl with dimples who taught Fatema a lot about Ugandan customs and called her Akiki, meaning "a friend". Florence's father was a doctor and she too wanted to be a doctor. All the teachers were nuns, Sister Etheriidae, the Maths teacher was Fatema's favourite teacher. Fatema excelled in all subjects, Maths being her favourite. She would receive perfect grades and would shine brighter than a star when the teachers would call out her name.

Fatema loved science and joined The British Red-Cross Society and received certificates and badges. During Christmas time every year, the Red Cross Society arranged visits to Leprosy Settlement to give them gifts of soap, toothbrushes, and medical needs that they required. Fatema remembered distributing them. The village/settlement had a school for the leprosy children, her teacher told her that the settlement was funded by The British Red Cross to give them what best life they can offer. They provided medication to help contain their disease and help ease the condition because there is no cure for leprosy; while treatment stops leprosy progressing, it can't reverse disability.

Fatema wanted to help humanity with all her might and would get worried and upset that she could not. There was a reason why she wanted to become a doctor as a child.

Leprosy is spread by moisture droplets from untreated leper through the air. It would take years of living close to an untreated leprosy patient to catch the disease. You cannot get leprosy from casual contact with a person who has the disease, like shaking hands or hugging, sitting next to each other on the bus or sitting together at a meal.

Around 95% of people are thought to be naturally immune. But when immunity is lowered due to poor nutrition, illness, and general living conditions, people are more likely to catch leprosy. The researchers determined that leprosy originated in East Africa or the Near East and travelled with humans along their migration routes, including those of trade in goods and slaves.

St Anne's School arranged lots of excursions to factories in nearby towns. Fatema remembers a trip to a cotton factory. Sacks of cotton handpicked from the cotton plantation are harvested by hand to remove the seeds before they are brought into the factory. Cotton seeds are sold as livestock feed, particularly for dairy cows. The fluffy cotton is brought into the factory, washed, spun into thread; then it goes through the weaving process and woven into material. It is then dyed into different colours, machine dried cut, and stitched into garments such as shirts, dresses, and trousers, all packaged and sent to be sold in shops.

Visitors can also visit the tea plantation in Toro district, located at the foothills of Mount Rwenzori. The guided tour starts from Kibale National Park to a hilly green landscape covered with miles of tea plantation, the greenness of the plantation that is dotted with large trees and the countryside freshness is relaxing. Large trees, like silver oak trees are regularly planted on tea plantations to regulate the soil ecology and filter the strong sun rays. The soil should be permeable, loose, and deep since the tea plant's roots can push down to a depth of up to 6 meters.

The guide will strap you with a harvest basket on your back and a hat strap on the head to hold the basket. Tea is harvested by hand. Not all leaves are plucked (picked), but only a few top young and juicy leaves with a portion of the stem. After the tea leaves have been plucked, the fresh leaves are first taken to a tea factory. The next stage is the sorting process of making black tea. Leaves are separated according to the particle size using sieves, and then the tea is cleaned by a process called solar withering to remove dust. Before they leave the tea factory, all the tea is graded and sorted. Because different sized leaves brew at different speeds, the leaves are separated into batches of the same size and "oxidated". Oxidation is a process through which tea leaves are exposed to the air in order to dry and darken, contributing to the flavour, and strength of different teas.

Making black tea is a simple process. This type of tea is allowed to fully ferment before drying. Oxidising changes the chemical constituents in the tea leaves, and this results in different brews.

The processes of tea manufacture produce three major types of tea: green tea that is unfermented, oolong tea that is semi-fermented and black tea that is fully fermented. There are only 24 hours between the moment the tea leaves are plucked and the minute they are packed up. But what happens during these 24 hours is crucial, as this is when the destiny of the leaves will be determined.

The process of removing caffeine by using ethyl acetate is often labelled as "naturally decaffeinated" since this chemical occurs naturally in tea leaves.

The guide explains that tea is an energy drink with 200 mg of caffeine, but is sugar-free, has vitamins A, B, C and E in the drink, so it is all healthy and good.

All students had a tasty cup of tea with added sugar in disposable paper cups.

Another excursion St Anne's school organised was a trip to the neighbouring country to the Democratic Republic of Congo to a city called Goma that is on the Ugandan border. Congo was a Belgian colony in central Africa and was known as Belgium Congo from 1908 until its independence in 1964. The Democratic Republic of Congo is named after

The Congo River, which flows throughout the country and is the deepest river in the world, and the world's second-largest river by discharge; Amazon being the first largest. The students and teachers travelled by bus and stayed overnight in a school dormitory. They were given a warm welcome, food and accommodation were provided by the education authorities. Such exchange of students' visits/travels were common in African boarding schools.

They had a tour around the beautiful city and visited the museum. Fatema's French teacher acted as a guide. French is the official language widely spoken around the country. Other languages like Swahili and other Bantu languages are also spoken by the locals.

Whilst at Teachers Training College, Fatema remembers a visit to Madhwani Sugar Factory in Kakira, Jinja, a town near Kampala, the capital city of Uganda. It is now called

Kakira Sugar Works. All the girls and the tutors travelled in a huge van as they sang songs on the journey. They were welcomed and were given plastic overalls, a hat and shoes covering at the entrance, and were escorted into the factory. On observation, they saw sugarcane brought in huge trucks; the cane stalks are washed, shredded, and juice squeezed out at the sugar mill. The juice is purified, filtered, and then boiled. It is then spun to remove impurities to separate the sugar crystal from molasses. The brown liquid, all girls tasted, was overly sweet; the juice is converted into brown sugar, packaged, and transported to be sold as brown sugar. Most of the sugarcane juice is refined into white sugar that is also packaged and sold.

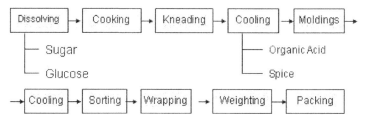

All the students were then taken to the Sweet Factory, where white sugar is dissolved under heat and cooked, and organic Acid/spice is added for flavour, next is the process of kneading, and moulding. Sweets turned into different colours, flavours and shapes are individually wrapped in clear paper, all done by machines and filled into jars or packaged and transported to be sold in local shops. The observers, students and teachers were given lots of sweets.

At lunch time, a meal of potato curry and puri was given by the factory owner Mr Muljibhai Madhvani.

The next visit also in the city Jinja. The Owen Falls Dam now called Nalubaale Power Station is a hydroelectric power station across the White Nile near to its source at Lake Victoria. Nalubaale is the Luganda name for Lake Victoria. The dam was built to produce electricity.

In 1947, Charles Redvers Westlake, an English engineer, reported to the Colonial Government of Uganda recommending the construction of a hydroelectric dam at Owen Falls near the city of Jinja. This led to the establishment of the Uganda Electricity Board (UEB).

The consultant engineer on the project was Sir Alexander Gibb & Partners. Eighty thousand tons of plant and construction materials, including 36,000 tons of cement, were shipped out from Europe in the difficult post-war period. They were then hauled 750 miles by rail from

Mombasa to Jinja. The dam was completed in 1954. It supplies electricity to Uganda and parts of neighbouring Kenya and Tanzania.

The thunderous noise of the water falling through the dam is deafening but a fascinating experience. The wet, fine mist spray from the waterfall could be felt by the passers-by, which was pleasant in the mid-day heat. Fatema and the other few girls were taken through wooden doors at the bottom of the dam; the original Power Station, to see how power is produced. When water is released through the dam, it spins a turbine connected to a generator that produces electricity. The water returns to the river on the downstream side of the dam. The power station consisted of a concrete gravity dam with a close-coupled intake powerhouse unit. It controls Lake Victoria's outflow through a series of turbines and sluices that are in the dam. When fully opened, generating capacity gradually increases. It supplies electricity to the whole country and the neighbouring countries.

Fatema's school also arranged a trip to a peach orchard where peaches grew on trees. When ripened, they were picked, washed, peeled, processed, and canned in syrup. Everyone had a taste of fruit in sweet syrup. The exposure Fatema received from such school trips helped her become well versed in many different things and opened up her interest in various subjects.

Kinyamasika TTC was an all girls Teachers Training College. The uniform was a blue skirt, white blouse. After completing four years of Teacher's Training, she went on two-year probation years as a qualified teacher in all black boys' primary school, where she was constantly observed by inspectors from the Department of Education. After that, Fatema was awarded a Teacher's Certificate.

Fatema was offered a place in the Asian primary school, her very first primary school that she had attended herself. Here she introduced the British Red Cross Society to junior students and took on evening games and sports, arranged netball tournaments with other African schools. Within a year of being at the school, Fatema won head-master's 'Best Teacher Award'. Fatema was awarded a two year, full pay up-grading course in Shimoni Teachers' Training College in conjunction with Makerere University in Kampala, the capital city of Uganda.

She stayed in the hostel there and mingled with lots of friends, mainly Agakhani and Hindu girls and boys. Fatema was born a Muslim, her upbringing had a very strong Islamic influence. She never missed prayers, fasts, and followed all religious rituals strictly. She believes Shia Islam is the true and the best religion. She was shy, mixed with both girls and boys, never strayed from her firm religious beliefs.

There was a boy, Rustam, a year younger than Fatema, who told her that he had mentioned Fatema as a marriage partner to his mother who was adamant that she wanted him to "marry someone younger." This was a cultural requirement. A man had to be older than a woman. Fatema told him that her 'father has got someone older' in mind for her. As a custom, she wanted her parents to arrange introduced marriage to a suitable boy. Rustam had an older brother Anwar who was a qualified secondary school teacher. Rustam's parents approached Fatima's father, who redirected him to Fatema's cousin Maria, who came from India and was two years older than Fatema. Within a few months, they were married.

Whilst at Shimoni TTC, she met with Rubina, a student at the college who invited Fatema for tea at her house where she met with Rubina's brother Shiraz who Fatema thought was younger than her and took no notice of him.

Fatema's older sister, Sukyna, who was two years older, completed her teacher's college and joined Fatema at the Asian School. The name of the school changed to Mpanga School as there were more black Ugandan students enrolling at the school, and was now government-funded. Fatema worked at the school and on weekends and evenings she also did tutoring. She worked hard, she enjoyed working as she believes that its better to be busy than bored.

The headteacher, Mr Singh, thought Fatema was older than Sukyna because she completed college before Sukyna. In the school, they were the only two Asian teachers, the other two were Norwegians, and the rest were black Ugandans.

An incident occurred at school when one day Mr Singh, the headteacher, called Fatema in his office, requested her presence in a sentimental meeting with a school child. 'I want you to be a witness in a meeting, as you are an Asian and this nine-year-old Asian girl wants to talk to someone.' The girl was crying, she was scared, and told Fatema that she was raped by Mr Toor, her neighbour, a married man who was a father of two. She said he offered her sweets and took her in the outhouse; she was not to tell anyone. The incident started when she was seven. The neighbour, Mr Toor, was brother in law of the headmaster's wife, Mrs Jasveen Singh, who was also a school secretary. Therefore Mr Singh wanted Fatema to keep quiet about the incident and Fatema was sworn to secrecy. At this stage, Fatema, very naïve, had no knowledge of sex did not know what 'rape' meant. Fatema decided to forget all about it and told no one.

Fatema frequently had sore throat, laryngitis/tonsillitis, which she thought was because of vocal use in teaching; she needed tonsillectomy an operation for sore throat. Her sister Rukaya, a student nurse at Mulago Nursing Hospital, arranged the tonsillectomy for Fatema.

Fatema was admitted to a children's ward as that was the only available bed at the time. It was sad to see little children so ill; their mothers by their bedside praying for their recovery. Fatema's bed was next to a four-year-old little girl Noora, the most beautiful little girl, she looked like a doll and was very chatty; her mother told Fatema that she had cancer of the kidney and was awaiting her operation; Fatema prayed for her recovery. Fatema said she was to keep her distance as her sore throat may be contagious. Her mind went to the little girl's suffering and how she wanted her to get better. She did not deserve all the pain at such a tender age. She wished and prayed she would get healthy immediately and thanked God for the health of her family.

Fatema was advised to 'fast after midnight before your tonsillectomy.' This means you should not drink or eat. An empty stomach reduces the risk of feeling nauseous from the anaesthetic.' The next day she was given an anaesthetic, the surgery was performed, and she was in the ward. A nurse was at her side trying to wake her up. When she did wake up, she thought it was the most painful experience of her life. Her throat hurt too much! It was like her throat had consumed fire the way it was burning. She found it difficult to inhale and exhale or even move her head. With each passing second, the pain was becoming unbearable. She was to gargle some mixture to ease the pain and was also given pain killers that made her drowsy, so she slept most of the time. Significant rest is imperative for at least the first forty-eight hours after a tonsillectomy, and all normal activities should be limited. Activity can then increase slowly and gradually.'

After two days in the hospital, her pain eased, and she was discharged. Rukaya, Fatema's sister arranged a taxi for her to go home.

Fatema enquired about the little girl Noora, Rukaya said she went home after her operation. Once again Fatema prayed for little Noor to get better.

Fatema's young life revolved around people she cared for, and strangers she had come to care for.

Fatema was advised that most adults have immense throat pain for one to two weeks or longer. The pain may get worse before it gets better. Fatema was told the pain in her throat might also make her ears hurt. Of course, Fatema was also ready for her entire face to be in discomfort, if not plain agony. She was further advised chewing sugarless gum may help speed recovery after surgery.

Chapter 5

Ali, Fatema's father, had three brothers and two sisters, and their families who lived in India. Ali's mother also lived in India. Ali sent some money and invited his oldest brother Kassam with his family to Uganda. Kassam had a young son Raheem and three daughters, Khadija, Maria, and Hanifa.

Ali was thinking of his own daughters and thought it would be ideal if Raheem married his eldest daughter Banu, but Raheem, twenty-six, liked Sukyna, Ali's second daughter, who was twenty-three and was very attractive. The mosque regulations require birth certificates and documents to register the marriage. New birth certificates were created since they were all previously burnt down in the shop fires. Ali just guessed the dates to prepare the documents as, in those days, birthdays were never celebrated. Ali made up the dates maybe to align by lunar dates and put the older daughter Banu's date of birth in January, Sukyna's date in February, Fatema was March; the year too was just guessed.

Ali paid some money to the hospital administrator, who printed out copies of birth certificates as required/requested. That is how all documents got sorted in those days. You pay money to get what you want. Sukyna left her job as a teacher, was married to Raheem, and lived with her in-law's extended family, sharing all the house chores. This was common in Asian culture. Once women were married, they looked after the children and did all the household chores. Raheem worked in a shop at The Bhimani's Department Store. His father Kassam worked as an accountant for the same firm, The Bhimani's.

Ali's younger brother Abbas, who also came from India, was to teach Arabic Quran reading and religious values/stories to all the children in the family. Abbas went back to his family in India after three years; he was homesick and did not want his family to join him in Uganda.

Fatema's parents arranged for her to meet a suitable boy to be introduced to her. It turned out to be the same boy Shiraz she met at Rubina's house while at college. Her parents told her he is very religious and has a very good job with an English firm. Fatema, like any person, wanted her own family, so she accepted his proposal and soon afterwards, they were engaged. They exchanged correspondence regularly for six months. He seemed to be a good religious person. Fatema was twenty-four, and he was twenty-eight. They got married and went on a honeymoon for one week at a farm owned by his brother-in-law Jalal, who lived there with his wife, Maimuna, Shiraz's eldest sister, and their three children. Jalal's big farm had lots of fruit trees. He grew variety of vegetables and bred cows for milk; he had workers who looked after the farm and milked the cows. He supplied milk to the inhabitants of Fort Portal town.

After a week at the farm, they went to live in Shiraz's family's rented home in Kampala. It was traditional for all Muslim women to have arranged/introduced marriages and live with their husbands and extended families. Fatema lived with Shiraz's seven siblings and his parents. Eleven adults in a four-bedroom house.

Fatema immediately started helping with the house chores. She wanted to help and mingle with the family members and be accepted by all. But Shiraz and his father wanted her to get a job, bring money from her parents, and do all the house chores. They showed her a lot of cash that Shiraz's mother, Banu brought from her brothers' every time she visited them. The family car that Shiraz's father drove was bought with his mother's money that she received as an inheritance from her father after his death.

Shiraz and his father Ramzan wanted Fatema to bring a lot of money from her father so that "Shiraz can buy his own car and a house" or "We'll terminate this marriage." Both were threatening and bullying her. Fatema went to multiple schools with her documents. She had good references and awards from the headmaster of her previous job, so she applied for a teaching position in the nearest school to their home and was accepted, within a week she started teaching full-time, afternoon session 1 pm to 7 pm.

In the mornings, she was to help with the house chores, cooking, sewing, everything. All of Fatema's wages went into a joint account with her husband, Shiraz's. She had no access to her own earnings and was advised that Shiraz had to pay for the jewellery given to her and other wedding debts. Fatema had to pay for her own wedding and now his wedding debts too. And she was to bring money from her father as well. Fatema knew it was greed, but she didn't say anything to her father, who did not have anything to give; such exploitation is unbelievable and is unheard of. It was early days and Fatema wanted to save her marriage. She prayed that things would change once she starts a family of her own.

Shiraz's brother, Nizar, completed his A-Levels and went to London, UK, for further studies. He left for London in the 1960s before Fatema and Shiraz were married in 1971. His wealthy uncles, his mother's brothers financed him. He studied there and had a job as an accountant in a firm in London, UK.

Fatema remembers one incident where she did all the house chores and went to school to teach. When she came home in the evening, exhausted, carrying a pile of books to mark, there were forty children in her class. She also had to prepare lesson notes for the next day for the headmaster. She went straight into her room and nodded off. Her mother-in-law Banu woke her up harshly, saying, "You cannot sleep during Maghreb (evening prayers) times. It's not allowed in this house." Fatema apologised, but Banu was upset and wanted her dress done, saying, "You have to do alterations to my dress. You should have done it before you went to work."

Fatema took the dress and started doing the required alterations even when she had piles of books to mark. Banu complained to Shiraz, saying that she wanted to wear it today. She had brought lots more material for garments to be stitched. At that moment, Fatema wished that she had never learnt to sew. If she stitched clothes in the morning, Banu would complain to Shiraz that she never helped in the kitchen. She was never happy when Fatema stitched her clothes, she always faulted them!

Fatema's mother, Noor, did not stitch clothes. Her father Ali could sew clothes for his daughters, Fatema had taught herself to sew. She was excellent at sewing, knitting, crotchet, and all was self-taught. Fatema's love for art was so grand she used to sew her own clothes, knit sweaters and crotchet since she was eight years old.

End of the term school holidays, Fatema's father was called to take Fatema home to Fort Portal. Her husband and father-in-law had told her that she was to bring money from her father. Fatema's father always travelled in a taxi as he did not own a car, and public transport was not available/reliable.

At her parents' house, Fatema felt extremely sick. She later found out she was pregnant. When she told Shiraz, he did not say anything and refused to bring her back to his home at the end of the school holidays. Fatema's father Ali took her back to her in-laws' house in a taxi. Fatema's father could not afford anything, let alone give her money that her in-laws wanted. Her father owned a small shop and had to feed his own family. It was hard to make ends meet. Fatema was torn between wanting to please her insensitive money-hungry husband and her sweet, loving family's well-deserved and earned money. Still, she did not let them know of her husband's greed for money.

Fatema's father, Ali, was such a wonderful, caring person. Her uncle Shaban and Razaq, her sister Sukyna's husband, also her cousin Mariam's husband, were all so devoted, loving men. She thought all men would be like her father and look after her, but Shiraz and his father, who did not fear Lord God's punishment, were bullying and harassing Fatema. She thought of her Holy Book, the Quran. She specifically thought of a verse in Surah Baqarah 2:153, which says, *'Fear the non-believers, for they will harm you, they do not know the existence of God'.*

These people who were bullying her performed all religious rituals. They prayed, fasted, and went to the mosque regularly. They were believers but Satan, Devils, who had no fear of Lord God's punishment. Fatema prayed for protection from these devils.

Shiraz had a good job, and his father and brother and even his two sisters all worked and contributed to the family budget. Fatema also worked. They lived in the same house, were paid well, yet they wanted Fatema's father to provide money to them. Fatema's father was on his own, had debts and had nothing to spare. They did not seem to care for that. They were cold people who only cared for material wealth and did not bat an eye when they did injustice to an innocent woman.

Fatema was sick. She could not keep anything down, not even water, and felt hers would be a difficult pregnancy. She felt very weak. She visited a doctor who gave her some tablets to stop the sickness, but Shiraz was angry he scolded her for wasting money. Shiraz wanted her to continue working because he did not wish for her income to ever stop coming.

He even told her to get rid of the baby. "You have to continue with your job,"

He was thinking of the debts he had to pay and did not want an extra mouth to feed. He was not going to pay for either of them. He was very abusive and nasty. Fatema did not tell anyone about the abuse but prayed that she would have a boy so things would change.

Mariam, Ali's fifth daughter, completed her junior secondary education, went to Kampala for higher education, and after that went to university (Hospital) Southampton, UK, to study Radiography.

Shiraz's sister Rubina, who was the same age as Fatema, had her marriage arranged to Zain, a wealthy businessman from London, UK. Zain was the same age as Rubina.

Rubina asked Fatema to share her clothes and jewellery with her and with her other sisters. Fatema willingly gave them her saris, gold jewellery, whatever they wanted. Rubina wore Fatema's pink sari for her engagement ceremony. Fatema was the bridesmaid for Rubina's wedding ceremony, both of which took place in the mosque. Rubina went to live in London, UK, and her husband paid for her travels and all her expenses. She never worked after she was married.

When the baby girl Amana was born, Fatema was on six-week maternity leave. Her father was called by Shiraz's father to take her home to Fort Portal and told Fatema that she was not to come back if she did not bring money from her father. She also was to return to her full-time job. In the era where women looked after their family, his own married sisters did not ever work. Shiraz and his father bullied her and humiliated her for producing a girl and for not bringing cash compared to her mother-in-law's cash 'gifts' that she received every time they visited her wealthy brothers, who lived in Mbale District. His father said Ali should give money to his Thee (means daughter in Asian language). His mother was not keen to look after baby Amana, she wanted Shiraz to pay for a maid/servant to help her with the baby and the house chores; a male servant already helped with washing, ironing, cleaning, shopping, and house chores. Everyone had servants. Shiraz hated paying for anything. He lied to Fatema that he was paying the rent of the house, and all his earnings were born into the rent.

Therefore, Fatema had to work. Her mother-in-law asked Fatema to leave the job, but when Fatema said she was forced to work, the mother-in-law told her, "Never speak adversely of your husband." Fatema thought, "What husband? Shiraz is no husband." He refused to take responsibility to look after her or her child. He gave them nothing; he did not even pay for the wedding ring. All the jewellery was bought on a hire purchase (HP), also known as an instalment plan, which is an arrangement whereby a customer agrees to a contract to acquire an asset by paying an initial instalment and repays the balance of the price of the asset plus interest over a period of time.

Shiraz made Fatema pay for everything. He paid the jewellers from her wages; she had no access to her own earnings as he controlled her income. She was completely at his mercy, and he was a heartless and inconsiderate excuse of a man. He had a family, a wife, and a daughter, yet he did not seem to care for their livelihood and was only interested in money. He did not care where that money came from; if it was the blood, sweat, and tears of the wife, he was indifferent about it.

He never thought of Amana as his child. He referred to her as Fatema's daughter. After the maternity leave that Fatema had spent at her parents' home, her father paid for her taxi costs and all the expenses. She was to go back to work when she returned to her husband's family home. She was very weak but had no choice, so she returned to work. There were maids and servants to look after Amana and do all the house chores.

Shiraz's second sister Zahra was attractive and had a lovely personality was married to Roshan, a big man, they lived in Tanzania. Zahra visited the family with her five-month-old baby daughter, Ruby. They came by plane. Zahra's husband would not let his wife and baby travel long, tiring journey by road. He looked after his family well. They always travelled by plane in comfort. Zahra brought her daughter's clothes for Amana as Ruby had outgrown them.

Fatema happily accepted them as readymade clothes were expensive' she had to sew baby clothes for her daughter, and was also happy to learn technics of motherhood from Zahra. Her husband was a good cook and loved food. She said he always helped her in the kitchen. In fact, he did most of the cooking. Zahra and her daughter stayed for a few weeks and left by return flight. Listening to Zahra narrate the kind-hearted personality that her husband was, Fatema felt happy for her but also disliked her own husband more for not giving her the basic rights and care that she deserved. Yet, Fatema was a patient and God-fearing woman. She knew this was not how her life would always remain.

Just then, there was a political turmoil in Uganda. President Milton Obote was out of the country attending a summit with other heads of government on 25 January 1971 while Obote was attending a Commonwealth summit meeting in Singapore, Idi Amin launched a coup when he learned that Obote was planning to arrest him for misappropriating army funds. Uganda Army and military police force, loyal to Amin, moved to secure positions in and around capital city Kampala, and Entebbe, Uganda's International Airport.

Chapter 6

Sporadic firing of automatic weapons and a few mortars continued until about midday. It was utter mayhem all around. Radio Uganda broadcasts gave the country the news of an apparently successful coup. President Milton Obote, who was flying back home from the Commonwealth conference as the coup took place, arrived in Nairobi, Kenya, the neighbouring country, that night. The news of Obote's deposition had brought Kampala people cheering into the streets. They strewed green branches before army vehicles, cheering, drinking, and dancing with troops, who continued firing celebration volleys into the air.

A broadcast by an unnamed army officer accused President Obote and his regime of corruption. It claimed that the President was suppressing democracy and failing to maintain law and order. The anonymous man also alleged the former President had insulated Uganda from Kenya and Tanzania. Perhaps the most significant allegation was that he tried to divide the army and put his fellow Lango tribesmen in the senior most army and Government posts.

The authority imposed a night-time curfew from 9:00 pm till 6:00 am daily to curb violence and restrict people leaving their homes. Army soldiers were everywhere, ready to shoot. Amidst the political chaos and disturbance in the country, Fatema was forced to go to work. She thought if she was killed, Shiraz would have left Amana to the mercy of servants; he hated the female child.

Idi Amin was in power as head of the country. It was on 10th August 1972 that Amin declared all Asians must leave the country, giving the deadline of three months, by 10th November 1972. His announcement and policies ended up expelling over 80,000 Asians living in Uganda, most of who had British passports. They were mainly second-generation Indians whose parents were born in Uganda out of their grandparents who the early British colonial rule brought to Uganda.

The Asians who were settled there owned most of the businesses – Uganda was their home. The reason that Amin was extraditing them was to take over their businesses and wealth. **The ironic truth was that this hardworking, entrepreneurial community had fallen victim to its own success**. Most Asians were highly successful in their businesses and were very wealthy, which led to their downfall.

The key words which Amin used were:

"I am going to ask Britain to take over responsibility for all Asians in Uganda who are holding British passports, because they are sabotaging the economy of the country."

He also said there was "no room in Uganda" for these people who had decided not to take up local citizenship and accused them of "encouraging corruption." He said the emphasis must now be on jobs for Ugandans, especially those of African race.

This would be a tactful reference to the fact that a great many key posts in the public sector are still held by able people of Asiatic race. This causes resentment, even when these Asians have opted for Uganda citizenship since independence in 1962.

The feeling among the Africans is that the Asians gained a flying start in colonial times by virtue of their better education and better command of English. By the time Britain handed over, the middle and upper echelons in commerce, the Civil Service and the professions were dominated by Asians. Some of the latter took local citizenship, while the majority opted for the British passports offered to them.

The pressure to give these jobs to Ugandans, produced an inevitable outward flow of British Asians, whose only travel document is the restricted type of British passport, which does not give automatic entry into Britain.

During this period of exile, there was confusion amongst Asians. They were terribly anxious, perturbed and felt insecure about their future. Uganda was their home, after all. It was a shock for them to think that they were to leave their homes, properties, and businesses. There was not enough time to sell their businesses, but most of all, they were worried for their lives.

For no rational reason, the state had announced that all Asians have to leave their homeland that they have been settled in for generations. Such was the anxious state of the Asians, especially those with small children. They did not know where and what their next destination would be at the other end of the spectrum.

To make matters worse, these Asians were not allowed to take their own wealth or valuables, gold, or money they had earned. Their homes, their cars were all left behind. It was a depressing time. It was some consolation that the British High Commissioner in Uganda took the responsibility of airlifting all the British Asians out of the country. Meanwhile, a few groups were taken in by other countries.

The approximate figures are as follows:

Britain took 27,200 Refugees.

Canada took 6,000.

India took 4,500.

Kenya took 2,500.

Others were taken in by West Germany, Austria, Malawi, Australia, New Zealand, Sweden, Norway and Mauritia.

20,000 Asians were unaccounted for; speculation states they may have either been killed or might have made their own way to their destinations without governmental support.

All in all, Amin's expulsion of Asians was a madman's dream that amounts to a horrendous **crime against humanity.**

'Special Report YouTube - Last Indians to Leave Uganda' covers the historic event.[1]

The chaos that followed this exile ultimatum of 90 days ended up causing a stampede. Idi Amin was the reason for approximately thousands of people losing their lives and for around 80,000 Indians leaving Uganda by November 10th, 1972.

When asked about it, Amin stated that, 'He saw a dream in which Almighty Allah had instructed him to declare a so-called economic war by expelling the non-citizen Indians from Uganda because they were allegedly "milking the cow without feeding it".'[2]

---

[1] New Vision TV. (2017, November 4). *SPECIAL REPORT - The Last Indian to leave Uganda* [Video]. YouTube.
https://www.youtube.com/watch?v=XkbfN3wiu74

[2] ThamesTv. (2016, September 3). *Uganda | Idi Amin | Asian Expulsion | 1972* [Video]. YouTube.
https://www.youtube.com/watch?v=p-i0JVip9N4

90 days were not enough. Asians were queuing up for their documents, collecting forms for entry to different countries, mainly to UK. It was a challenge to even withdraw money from the banks to buy flight tickets. They had very little time to get out of the country. If they didn't evacuate, they would face the concentration camp.

This was a fascist rule at play here. Amin was even reported to have said to a German official that Hitler was right in killing fifty million Jews. This evoked fear in many hearts. Everyone was worried The Madman Amin might order the killing of all the Asians at any time!

Among those who were evacuating were Shiraz's parents and all his siblings. Soon after Amin's announcement, they left for Entebbe International Airport, taking their personal belongings, and were airlifted from Entebbe International to Stanstead Airport in England. From there, they were taken to a refugees' camps in Gaydon. The UK government supported the migration, so they vacated army barracks to temporarily accommodate the refugees from Uganda.

Fatema and Shiraz were left in Kampala to continue their work until the end of the month. This meant she would get paid for that month, and all Shiraz wanted was money. He said to Fatema, 'Your wages for that month, October 1972, was not paid.' Shiraz is telling Fatema this in 2020. All he ever thinks and thought about is money/or financial loss. Fatema reflected herself that she never had access to her money anyway. Shiraz always took the lot.

1st November 1972 came, and Fatema with her 10-month-old baby Amana in her arms stood at Entebbe airport, waiting for the next flight out of Uganda. At customs, her luggage was checked inside out. She was not allowed to take any gold jewellery that she bought for her marriage and had paid for all herself. The officers confiscated the jewellery from the suitcase. Other pieces of jewellery survived because she had hidden them in between the clothes she was wearing. This was because Fatema was not physically checked since Amana was crying a lot. Hence, she managed to bypass some of the gold jewellery that she kept on her, hidden secretly in her clothes and under her belt.

Fatema boarded Sabena Airline, and so started her one-way flight to London, Heathrow, because she had a British passport. Shiraz had a Ugandan passport left after selling a few of his parents' belongings. He took all the money and bought tickets to India, Jeddah, Syria, and other middle eastern countries.

Fatema's flight to London was her first flight. She had never sat in a plane before, and was uncertain and scared for her little daughter's safety. There was a three-hour stopover at Brussels Airport for refuelling. By this time, Amana was very cold and unwell, she was crying. Fatema tried to feed her, but she did not want anything. Fatema could not change her either as the temperature was below freezing, and she feared Amana would catch a severe cold and become very ill.

Two Asian men who apparently sympathised with her condition approached her and offered to help with her hand luggage at the Brussels Airport. Fatema had never seen them before, so she refused their offer. They still continued to follow her. The two men boarded the plane without documents, saying to the air steward that they were with her, pointing to Fatema and baby Amana.

The plane landed at Heathrow airport on 2nd November. Everything was covered in snow and ice. The extremely cold temperature was a contrast in terms of climate in Uganda. The two men from Brussels who offered to help Fatema disappeared. They entered the UK as refugees from Uganda. She never saw them again.

Fatema and Amana had finally now entered the UK as refugees from Uganda. A team of British Red Cross who were awaiting Ugandan refugees assisted them to a room, with warm clothes and food and transported them to refugees camps at the Army Barracks that was vacated to accommodate the Ugandan refugees.

Both Fatema and Amana were too tired and cold, so they went to sleep as soon as they were shown to their room. The mother and baby slept for two days, such was their exhaustion. On the third day too, she was awoken by a knock at the door. When Fatema answered it, a lady appeared and told her that they had slept for two days and that she was concerned for their health/wellbeing.

Fatema learned that the lady was a nurse and needed to have some tests done on both. But Fatema excused herself for a while, saying that baby Amana needed to be fed and changed first. The weather was unbearably cold. Fatema wrapped Amana in a blanket, and soon they were given food and nappies and warm clothes.

Despite their best attempts, both Fatema and Amana contracted a severe cold and a bad cough. A doctor feared TB infection, checked them, and gave them some medication. They were then taken to a different refugee camp where they joined their in-laws. The authority, the benefits agency, gave them food, clothes and financial help. That money didn't reach Fatema either. Shiraz's father kept the money, and when Shiraz joined them a few months later, that's when he handed him Fatema's share.

After his arrival, Shiraz went for job interviews in factories. Being a non-white, it was difficult to get a job. The white British community generally did not want Asians in their country. They even carried out numerous demonstrations on the streets. Their slogans repeated saying, 'Pakies, Go Back to Your Own Country', all the while they were hurling food and rubbish at Ugandan refugees.

Meanwhile life in the camps continued. The local authority at the camps finally traced all the relatives. Rubina, Shiraz's sister and husband Zain from London visited the family. Shiraz's father, Ramzan asked for financial help from his son in law, Rubina's wealthy husband, Zain, but he could not offer any. Ramzan then tried his luck by visiting Shiraz's maternal uncles. These were Shiraz's mother's brothers, who used to be very wealthy businessmen in Uganda and in Karachi, but they also refused to give anything.

One of the uncles, Akbar, told Fatema that like everyone who left Uganda, they too were refugees and left everything they owned back home. 'Like everyone else, we are on social benefit and are living in a council house,' Akbar told Fatema, and asked her to explain it to her father-in-law that they could not welcome his family. When Fatema said she cannot pass on the message to her in-laws and that he would have to do it himself, so Akbar's wife Aunty Khadija did. They left empty-handed. The in-laws later discussed Aunty Khadija, saying that it is not her money, who is she to refuse them in this manner.

The housing authority eventually offered a council house to Fatema and her child. As expected, Shiraz's parents and siblings also wanted to be with him, so they all were given a bigger, four-bedroomed house in a village named Kirton near Ipswich.

Shiraz started a job in a nearby factory, iron smelting, where he was making car components. Fatema got an evening and weekend night-time job in a hospital as an auxiliary nurse.

The neighbours, the village people, were informed in advance of the Ugandan refugees' arrival and were all very friendly towards them. They wanted to help them settle down in their village. Some were curious and wanted to know what part of India was the country Uganda in. When Fatema told them, Uganda is in East Africa and was a British colony, and English language was the medium of instruction, they were surprised. Ladies wanted to know about her skin colour being brown; Fatema further explained that her grandparents were originally from India. The village ladies then invited Fatema to a 'coffee morning' for a chat. Fatema talked to them all and told them that she was a trained teacher. Fatema was invited to women's knitting/sewing groups, mainly aimed for beginners. She told them that she was a good craftsman and that she could knit, crotchet and knew how to sew clothes. Her experience with knitting sweaters and she could follow knitting patterns, since they were all friendly people. When they learned that Fatema was a Muslim and could not eat pork, her meat had to be halal (like Jews), they were shocked. Fatema explained that she had to read ingredients on even biscuit packets before she could consume them.

The family living opposite to her included Mary and John who had a daughter, Faith, the same age as Amana. Mary visited them often, and the two girls sharing toys but speaking different languages was fascinating. Amana was fluent in the Asian language that was her mother tongue. Mary wanted her daughter to learn the Asian language meanwhile, Amana would pick up English from her new friend. Since Uganda was a British colony with English as the main language anyway, Amana had picked some of it up in time to start a nursery school education.

Soon, Shiraz's father called Fatema's father Ali to keep Fatema and her child with him. As there were no maids to look after Amana, they told Fatema not to come back without money from her father, but Fatema told Shiraz that her father didn't have any. Shiraz said, "Your father has transferred a lot of money via your sister to Ali's fifth daughter who was studying in the UK" Fatema said, 'He did not have any money to transfer." She pointed out that his sister Maimuna who was married to Jalal always brought lots of fruits, vegetables, and dairy products from their farm. She asked Shiraz if his father had ever given anything to his daughters?

This made Shiraz furious! He swore using 'B'/'F' words. Shiraz's father this time wrote to Fatema's father to take her and not to bring her back. The letter stated that Fatema "has no respect for an old man, she is answering back to her father-in-law." Fatema had not done so, but women are always blamed for everything.

Chapter 7

Fatema's father did arrive in a coach from Southampton to pick up Fatema and Amana, who was nearly two. He bought a coach ticket for Fatema, and they travelled to his council house by bus. Fatema told her father that her in-laws think that he has transferred a lot of money to England via Mariam, who left Uganda a year before for further study in the UK. "So, they want your money." Fatema's father could not believe her! It was unbelievable for him that religious people like her in-laws would do that! Fatema stayed at her parents' house with all her siblings, her parents looked after Amana while Fatema went to work as a shop assistant in Owen & Owen Department Store.

Fatema was tasked to put price stickers on goods that were to be sold in the store. She was told very strictly never to go into the department store, and to stay in the back of the goods store to do her tasks. The two white girls working with her were to take the goods into the main department store.

Once, it so happened that one of the white girls was absent from work, presumably on sick leave. The other girl told Fatema that she was to help her lift the goods into the department store. Fatema helped her with a few large boxes when suddenly the manager entered and snatched the box from her. He told her that she should never be seen in the department store. This was because "the customers do not like seeing 'coloured people' handling goods."

Four months later, Fatema's father Ali wrote to Shiraz's father, persuading him to take Fatema back to her house in Ipswich; the council house was for Fatema and her one-year-old child Amana, but the father-in-law had thrown them out. It is an Islamic practice where it is crucial to save a marriage. Ali being a religious man, was doing his best to 'help' save the marriage. He had other daughters' reputation to think about. She was 'returned' to her in-laws in Ipswich. Fatema's father, Ali, paid for the coach ticket. He also gave some money to Shiraz, saying that they haven't got any more, as they were on social benefit. Fatema was not aware of this until 2019 when Shiraz said to Amana, 'Nana Ali gave me the money she, your mum, paid to Nani for your keep.' He never gave the money to Fatema; this shows his lust for money, consumed Fatema's hard-earned money.

Whoever loves money
never has enough;
whoever loves wealth
is never satisfied with their income.
This too is meaningless.
Ecclesiastes 5:10

Timothy 6:10, "For the love of money is a root of all sorts of evil.

Five months later, Fatema's in-laws moved to Birmingham to be nearer to the community, their mosque, and to the Muslim diet. Asian foods were not available in the village where they lived. Shiraz stayed on working in the factory, and Fatema had her weekend night-time job in the hospital in Ipswich. A year later, Shiraz applied for jobs in Birmingham. He was offered one with Royal Mail sorting office in Birmingham. They put their names down for council-house exchange scheme, and once the offer was accepted, they moved to Birmingham.

After that, Fatema's second daughter, Tahera was born. Fatema called the ambulance to take her to the hospital while Shiraz took three-year-old Amana to his mother to look after her. Fatema was in the maternity hospital for 24 hours and was discharged; she called a taxi from the hospital to her house that cost her £1.50, which infuriated Shiraz. He was always angry at her spending money. "You could have walked home" he said, "it's only a mile and a half from hospital."

Fatema had stitches, she was weak, and had a new baby in her arms, but she said nothing! Shiraz, swearing, refused to provide food for the mother and the baby. Fatema was very weak but was forced to breastfeed against doctor's advice. She was given vitamin D injections/tablets. The midwife who visited her told her that she 'would talk to

Shiraz' as Fatema was very weak and the child would not have enough milk. Fatema said it was not necessary. She prayed for God to provide milk for her child. For a woman who had just given birth, receiving such treatment was horrendous. She was not allowed to access her own earnings from the joint account and was told to bring money from her parents, who always gave her whatever they could afford.

Shiraz's parents visited the new baby empty-handed. Fatema had to cook for them, wash up, etc. His father said to Fatema that she had to return to work as 'Shiraz is not going to feed your daughters.'

Shiraz's sister Rubina who was married to Zain, a wealthy businessman from London, both with their two-year-old daughter also named Amana, visited the baby and brought a few expensive toys for Fatema's baby. They had called their daughter Amana because Zain liked the name Fatema's first daughter had, who was the cutest and the most beautiful child they had seen. Fatema's daughter Amana had light brown hair and hazel eyes.

Soon enough, Fatema's parents and siblings also visited the new baby Tahera and gave her some baby clothes and money. Shiraz took the money from her, saying he would buy premium bonds for them. She was shocked and said she needed nappies for her daughter. All her complains went in vain. He took the money and said, 'Money is not for you to spend.' He indeed bought premium bonds and said they will win a lot of money. They never did.

Fatema, out of desperation, was forced to ask the neighbours to give her their old terry nappies and clothes that they did not need. She also went to jumble sales, where she got second-hand clothes that she would handwash before making Tahera wear them. She did not have a washing machine for three years. Fatema even handwashed the sheets, towels, all clothing for everyone in the bathtub. Shiraz would not even wash his own underclothes, he would not lift a finger. On top of that, he would swear and hit her if she ever asked him to take his plate to the kitchen sink. The only child benefit she received was £1.98 per week for her second child. The first child did not receive anything.

Fatema was unable to claim any state benefits as the husband was earning enough. Still, he did not want to provide for his unwanted family. At this point, Fatema resolved she had to do something for her finances and started selling Avon cosmetics and jewellery door to door to feed her children.

With children in the pram, she was selling up to £500 net worth a month, which earned her 20% of the net sales. She gave praise to the Lord, who finds a way to sustain all. Fatema and her children's clothes were either given or bought from jumble sales that only cost a few pence. Fatema also went to a local market where material cost a pound for three meters. She was a good tailor and also started making clothes at home using a used sewing machine that was given to her by an old lady in Ipswich.

Fatema used to sell a lot of cosmetics in her community gatherings at the mosque; this boosted her income. Shiraz's sisters and his mother ordered a lot of cosmetics but were unhappy to pay her. When she asked for payment, they were offended. She agreed to give them 20% off, but even that was like 'drawing blood from a stone.'

Shiraz's sister Zahra from Tanzania, with her three daughters and big husband Roshan, occasionally visited her siblings and her maternal family who were settled in Birmingham, UK. Zahra loved Avon cosmetics and ordered a lot of it; Fatema had to give her whatever she wanted. Zahra and her husband being good cooks did all the cooking for her maternal family while they stayed with them. Fatema visited Zahra and her family; Zahra was advised to 'hide' the recipes. Shiraz said to her, "Don't show her your recipes."

Shiraz told Fatema that his sisters and his mother 'were the best cooks in the world.' Fatema agreed and said, "That's their full-time job; they don't go out to work or earn a living. Your sisters' husbands, unlike you, are good cooks and do all the house chores."

"She's jealous" is all he could say, and all would laugh at his 'jokes.'

When Tahera, Fatema's second daughter, was five months old, both Amana and Tahera were covered in chickenpox. They were unwell, so Fatema stayed at home. Just then, Shiraz's father died of a sudden heart attack at the age of sixty-five; Fatema could not attend, but Shiraz forced her to go to the in-laws' to help his mother in the kitchen as there were visitors. "All my uncles and relatives are 'asking of you,'" she was told.

Fatema attended their house with both her daughters covered in spots. She explained to the guests about the children being unwell. In Shiraz's family and community, in general, they looked down on women who produce girls. They treated them like slaves and felt sorry for the father. His aunt from Canada advised him to 'kick her out' because, in many cases, women are divorced for producing girls. Fatema knew that it is the male chromosome that determines the sex of the child. She had tried to explain it to Shiraz, but he did not want to know. He was rude to her and treated her like a slave. Well, even slaves get fed and sheltered, whereas Fatema had to pay and provide for her family.

Shiraz's father always supported him and said that Shiraz was not responsible for Fatema's daughters. Fatema had to get money from her father just like Shiraz's mother did. They did not understand that Fatema's father, unlike his mother's brothers, was not wealthy. Ali, Fatema's father, did not even have a shop in Uganda. Fatema's sisters visited

Uganda in 2019, a year after Fatema and Arif's visit there; Fatema told them that it's the best country in the world. Her four sisters visited all the landmarks and physical features of Uganda that Arif and Fatema had visited.

Rukaya, Fatema's sister, paid a solicitor in Uganda as she wanted to know what her father Ali's assets were before he left the country. "He had no assets," they were told. Shiraz wanted to inquire via Arif how much money Nana Ali had, when Arif told him he had no assets, Shiraz said, "They are lying;" he wanted to see the proof of solicitor's findings. To date, he still wants Fatema's inheritance that she does not have.

Fatema's father-in-law is buried in the Handsworth Cemetery and Shiraz visits his grave regularly. He hates Fatema because her father, Ali, maybe older, is still alive. Shiraz being jealous is extremely rude and nasty to Fatema.

Years later, after being with different cultures, Fatema realised that English culture was the same as Asian, Arab, African, Chinese; they too preferred boys to girls and blamed it on women who produced girls. 'Poverty is not a crime, ignorance is!' Even now, in the 21st century, our society is ignorant and believes that if a family has girls, the family name will not carry over to the next generation, the male being the dominant carrier of the family name. How can anyone explain that a name is not important in God's book/Quran? It is the bloodstream that is carried over to the next generation for both sexes equally; DNA testing only reveals a general ethnic breakdown, not the name. Women don't have to adopt husbands' surnames.

In 1979, the Chinese government introduced the 'One-Child Policy' to control the increase in population, which was threatening the country's prospects for economic growth. Although it had introduced several birth control initiatives during the previous decade, there was a substantial increase in population.

This caused unexpected imbalances in the demographic development of the country. Due to a traditional preference for boys, large numbers of female babies ended up homeless or in orphanages, and in some cases, were killed. "In the year 2000, it was reported that 90% of foetuses aborted in China were female." As a result, the gender balance of the Chinese population has become distorted. Today, it is thought that men outnumber women by more than 60 million!

Chapter 8

Fatema's sister, Mariam, who is Ali's and Noor's fifth daughter, had left Uganda a few months before Amin's expeltion of Asians from the country, met Imtiaz when she arrived in the UK. Imtiaz helped her find a place/student's accommodation with an old lady who had advertised a spare room in the university newsletter. Mariam completed her studies and worked in the hospital as a radiographer. Imtiaz also worked in the same hospital and was her senior work colleague. Imtiaz helped find accommodation – a council house for Mariam's parents and siblings; he also found a council house for his own parents and siblings, who all came to the UK as refugees, and were victims of Idi Amin's expulsion of mass exodus from Uganda.

Imtiaz was a good, responsible, caring person and both Mariam and he got on very well together. Imtiaz being a Sufi Muslim and Mariam being a Shia, the parents objected to the marriage in the first instance, but after persuasion from Uncle Shaban, both parents agreed. And with parents' blessings, the two were married. Fatema and her daughters attended the wedding. It was a small wedding at the bride's parents' home. A Muslim preacher from Bristol conducted the service. They were all happy, and a year later, they had a baby boy named Sajeed. He was a beautiful baby loved by all.

Two years later, Fatema had a baby boy, Arif, but then things got worse for her. Shiraz said, "You think I'll change because you've produced a boy? I will not give you a penny. I do not know who you have slept with and whose children they are." He said he did not know where she worked and what job she did. Fatema said she has a payslip from work showing where she worked and what her job role is; a weekend night-time job in the hospital as an auxiliary nurse. Shiraz neither acknowledged the kids as his children nor took an interest in them. Shiraz was a miser too tight feasted to feed his family; Fatema told him that he was worse than animals; then again, at least animals feed their own offspring.

Fatema was unaware that Shiraz told Amana, who was only eight, that "Mum is a bad woman. She wants money; I am going to commit suicide!" Amana was always crying silently/secretly, thinking Shiraz would die soon. He never did anything for them, but children did not know this. Whatever Fatema earned selling cosmetics was used for food, but Shiraz wanted Fatema to put it in the joint account that she had no access to.

***

Fatema's parents and siblings lived in a council house in Southampton that is a beautiful city. Ali Fatema's father worked in a factory that made balls from rubber/synthetic material; his eldest daughter, Banu, worked in a clerk shoe factory, sewing leather for shoes on sewing machines. The second daughter, Sukayna, did not work as she had to look after her four-year-old daughter Shabana and was pregnant with a second child when they left Uganda. Her baby boy Mustafa was born in Southampton Hospital later. Fatema's two brothers – at the time when they left Uganda Yasar, was sixteen, and Galeb, was ten - and the youngest sister, Tasneem, was twelve; they were enrolled in schools and thereafter in colleges/universities for further studies/training.

Fatema's sisters – Rukaya, who worked as a nurse in Southampton Hospital, and Mariam, who worked as a radiographer – had their own cars. They all went sightseeing and visited the city's main attractions.

The Port of Southampton is part of the largest UK shipping port and hub for passenger and cargo movement in South England. It carries over 34.5 million tonnes yearly and is the largest container port in the UK. It is noted as being the departure point for the RMS Titanic. 1,500 of the people perished on board Titanic on its maiden voyage in April 1912. Today there is a memorial park dedicated to the disaster with a large bronze replica of the ship's prow. Every April 15th, a historic church bell is rung 14 times. Everyone has heard the story of the band that played while the Titanic sank, but few thought to make a memorial for the musicians.

With large cruise and cargo ships coming and going, the view is conspicuous, especially good from The Hythe Ferry service that regularly runs across Solent, the 20-mile-wide river that separates the Isle of Wight from the mainland. Fatema, her children, and sisters visited the Isle of Wight with its beautiful sandy beaches. The landmark attraction is the Isle of Wight Pearl, The Needles, and Sandham Gardens.

Another place to visit highly recommended is Longleat Safari Park, where Fatema and the family visited with her sisters. They saw lots of East-African animals, including lions, tigers, rhinos, zebras, cheetahs, and many other animals and birds. They also visited Cheddar Gorge Craft Village; the entrance to Gorge is free, you can stop and take pictures with goats. An astonishing scenery it was! They visited the cave of aged cheddar cheese to sample a sensational taste of cheese. They also went to Weston Super-Mare Adventure Park, all great places to visit.

Fatema's parents Ali and Noor wanted to be near the community and the mosque, as well as near his brother Shaban and their relatives who lived in Croydon. Fatema's sister Rukaya, who was a nurse, looked for a property and a job in a hospital nearby. They all moved into Rukaya's five-bedroom house in Croydon, South London. There was no Mosque, but there was a rented community centre where all gathered for prayers. Ali and brother Shaban wrote to the World Federation for funds to build or buy a mosque/community centre there. They also travelled to various cities in the UK to raise funds. They managed to raise enough funds to buy an old Synagogue church building that was for sale and named it Husseinia Islamic Centre, where all Muslims united to congregate for prayers and other services/rituals.

Fatema's sister Sukayna was to move to Canada to join her husband, who was in Canada after the expulsion of Ugandan Asians and was settling/working in Montreal.

During the school holidays, Fatema and her children travelled by coach to London to visit Sukayna and bid farewell to her and her two children, who lived with her parents and siblings in Corydon before Sukayna and her children departed for Montreal. Fatema and her children stayed with them for a week. They decided to go two days sightseeing in London by bus and took a packed lunch with them during their stay there. They bought a bus day-pass each and visited Buckingham Palace, and they watched the changing of the guards, followed by having a picnic lunch in the palace garden. The next day they went to see Madam Tussauds, the waxwork museum of over 200 famous and historical lifelike figures and characters that look unbelievably live.

 They also visited The Trafalgar Square; the name commemorates the Battle of Trafalgar, the British victory in the Napoleon wars over France and Spain that took place off the coast of Cape Trafalgar in 1805. The pigeons fascinated her children; they were feeding the pigeons directly from their palms.

Shuffling, flapping mobs of pigeons were once as much a part of the Trafalgar Square experience at Nelson's Column and the National Gallery. But since July 2003, when former London mayor Ken Livingston introduced hawks to scare them off, numbers have tumbled, from 4,000 to just 120. Feeding Pigeons became illegal. Studies found that bird droppings and feathers can lead to diseases, such as histoplasmosis, candidiasis and cryptococcosis, which can be fatal in some cases.

■■

Fatema's uncle Shaban died prematurely at the age of 57 on his way home from work. Shaban owned a shop, and on that particular evening, he finished work, locked up, and was walking home. On the way home, he curled up and died; a passer-by called an ambulance that took him to the hospital. They traced his family from the papers and items in his pocket. Fatema's father, Ali was devastated. He said he had lost his son; he referred to Shaban as his son. Fatema and her children went to the funeral by coach. He was Fatema's favourite uncle. May he rest in peace.

Thereafter, Ali visited Shaban's grave every day to offer prayers; he walked three miles to the graveyard and walked back home; he was a very fit man. He sobbed and said he had moved from Southampton to be near Shaban but did not have long to be near him. Ali being the older brother, thought he would die first, but his son and now his brother left this world before him. Ali dedicated his life to helping his community, like he did in Uganda, raising funds and arranging many religious preachers/ministers from abroad, mainly from India. He arranged for Urdu-speaking preachers to deliver sermons and preach Islam to community members and to their children.

Ali was healthy and well, but one day, his leg gave in. He had a blood clot and eventual vein/artery blockage in his leg. He could not breathe and was rushed into hospital, where after an operation he recovered from his first heart attack. He was advised that he would have to watch his diet of low fat and will have to continue his daily walks. He lived for another two years after the first attack but lost his life after the second heart attack at the age of seventy-two. He was a great man; he not only helped his community but also did a lot of house chores. It was a great loss to both his community and his family. Fatema thought of her father as the best person in the world. She knows he has gone to a better place and would be united with his son and brother Shaban. She grieves and prays for them every day and hopes she, too, would be united with them one day.

***

Fatema's eldest sister, Banu, was married to a man from her community; he was a good cook and always helped her with the house chores. He died of diabetes after twenty years of happy marriage. Rukaya, Fatema's sister, who is a nurse, did not marry. Her engagement did not work out as planned. Yasar and Galeb both are married and have two children each. Tasneem, Fatema's youngest sister, got married, and both her children are also happily married.

Fatema's mother, Noor, had a lovely personality, she lived in the same house with Rukaya, Yasar, his wife, their daughter, Galeb, his wife and their two children. Noor died at the age of eighty-three; she was healthy and fit till the last three months of her life when she developed stomach problems. She had stomach pain, felt bloated, and was diagnosed with ovarian cancer. Noor lived long enough to see her youngest son Galeb's children. Fatema's prayers extend to her mum, the wonder lady.

Uncle Shaban's wife, Aunty Rubab, lived till she was 82; she was a grandmother to all her four daughters and to her three sons' children. Fatema and her cousins are still good friends and keep in touch with each other and with all the cousins.

Shiraz's brothers and his work colleagues constantly borrowed money from him, but he refused to lend any, particularly to Fatema. Amana went to the local schools nearest to their home. She was a very bright child who started reading at the age of three. Her nursery teacher was astonished to see a three-year-old reading and writing short sentences. When in primary school, her teacher called Fatima to tell her that Amana would be put in a class ahead of her as she was answering all questions before other children could respond. After her primary, she went to the local secondary and completed her GCSE with high grades. She was a high achiever and also completed her A-levels with flying colours. For her university studies, Amana got a place at Birmingham University and was awarded a full grant from the local authority. She stayed at home, and she also worked weekends and school holidays at the Birmingham airport. She bought her own car, a mini-Fiat, to travel to and from university and work.

Tahera, the second daughter, did not get a place in Birmingham University; she went to the University of Greenwich, London. Fatema needed money for her daughter's accommodation, but Shiraz refused to lend it, saying, "I will not give you a penny! She should have done better at school. She is a failure." He was very abusive;

Tahera had passed with good grades but was unable to secure a place in a university near home. She was not a 'failure' as Shiraz had stated just to humiliate her; she had to borrow a student's loan. Fatema also re-mortgaged her own house to get extra funds from the bank and was paying endowment, interest-only mortgage. Tahera and Fatema managed to buy a two-bedroom flat in Ilford, East London. Tahera also worked weekends and school holidays.

Shiraz never bought anything for his children – no birthday or Eid presents for any of his own family. However, he bought gold necklaces personalised with their names in gold and other jewellery for all his brothers' daughters. Shiraz being the older brother wanted his younger ones to like and praise him. His brothers thought highly of Shiraz because they thought he was giving such expensive gifts to their daughters; he must be a good father to his own daughters! Shiraz said to Fatema, "You buy it for your daughters." He always referred to them as 'your daughters' or 'her daughters,' never as his. He said to Fatema, "I buy it for my brother's daughters because their wives don't work." His married sisters did not work either, which Fatema pointed out, but their husbands provided for them. Shiraz would not even feed his family, let alone shelter or clothe them. Fatema said to him, "I am unable to get any social benefits because you are supposed to provide for my family." He was worse than animals.

Fatema stopped talking to him and refused to provide for him. For twenty years, she was like a slave, doing everything for him. When they came from Uganda, in the refugee camps, and thereafter in a council house, there was no washing machine. Fatema did everything for him on her own. Shiraz did not even wash his own underwear and never lifted a spoon. She would ask him to take his plate to the sink and he would be livid! "Who do you think you are talking to? I don't do anything in this house!"

Shiraz was like a self-proclaimed king. He was nasty and abusive, and he knew that she would not divorce him because of two girls. In Asian culture, women are looked down upon when they are divorced, and no one is willing to marry the daughters of a divorced woman. But now, she decided to put an end to it.

Fatema was doing everything in her house washing, ironing, cooking, cleaning, gardening, looking after children, and going to work in the evenings and weekends. She went to coach house evening prep schools, tutoring students for 11+ exams and working at weekends, then working night-time job at Bartlett Hospital as an auxiliary nurse, and during daytime going door to door selling Avon cosmetics with baby Arif in the pushchair. She opened her own bank account, and when children all went to school, she worked a nine-to-three weekday job at Metropole Hotel, cleaning and preparing rooms for guests. She also continued with her weekend night-time job.

Fatema applied for a teaching position but was advised that her qualification was not recognised and would have to retrain and provide GCSE certificates in Maths and English. Fatema applied to the school's examination board to allow her to sit for exams in the two subjects; she passed them both. She had been helping Amana with her homework and knew that it would be easy to pass the exams without requiring any coaching. Uganda's education system was better than British education in terms of quality. What Fatema did in her 11+ exams at junior school in Uganda was equivalent to the GCSE in the British schools.

Fatema then applied for a training course at Birmingham Polytechnic. After several interviews with the lecturers and education department, she was given full recognition in writing of her Uganda teaching qualification and was advised to apply for teaching positions in schools. She did and had several interviews but was unsuccessful in securing a teaching position. She also tried for teaching assistant's job but was not successful because of her skin colour. She was literally told that there were too many white teachers waiting/queueing for primary teaching jobs. In one interview, a headmaster flashed a light on her face and said if you make a complaint, "It's your word against mine. No one will believe you!"

Fatema applied for driving lessons; in those days, it was £3 per lesson. She took six lessons and took a test but failed her first test; thereafter, she took further six lessons and finally passed her driving test, eventually buying her own car, a mini for £150. Later, when the children were older, she got a full-time job with PCT (Primary Care Trust) as a data quality clerk. She also worked with Tudor House Prep School as a tuition teacher on weekends.

Working seven days a week, she bought a better car. The council house they lived in was not in a safe area, and they were constantly broken into whilst they were away attending services in their mosque. The house was far from the community and the mosque; the family decided to look for a house closer to the mosque. They sold the council house and moved to a house nearer to their mosque, the city, and Amana's university. Fatema continued paying the mortgage, and the house's insurance as Shiraz refused to pay for anything.

Chapter 9

When Fatema's daughter, Amana, was 15, she had a weekend and holiday job at the airport working as a cashier. She was protected by a security guard as in her job, she was dealing with banking and finance. Amana finished her GCSE with good grades and went to Solihull Sixth Form College to study A-levels. She took driving lessons that her college offered to students at a subsidised concession price and bought a small Fiat to get her to and from the University of Birmingham.

In her third year, for her electives, she chose to go to Karachi. This was fully funded by her university. Fatema, her daughter Tahera, and her son Arif also accompanied Amana to Karachi as her university advised her for safety and warned against travelling on her own in a foreign country. For her elective subject, Amana chose the 'Consanguinity', a union between two individuals who are related as second cousins or closer. This study was to make public awareness on the prevention of congenital and genetic disorders in the offspring.

Fatema thought the weather in Karachi in July and August was extremely hot, but the people were genuinely nice and would bend down to help. Amana visited Baqai Medical University to get some information on her case study on her topic 'Consanguinity'. The research was spread over a period of six weeks and included a series of visits to schools, community centres, and mosques. There were several interviews with headteachers, recording disabilities in children and finding the cause of disabilities. Fatema could speak Urdu and Hindi, and accompanied Amana on all the visits. Most people spoke English as the medium of instruction.

They travelled in a three-wheeled cart called tuk-tuk, or auto rickshaws as they commonly call it. These are proper vehicles with an engine that are commonly seen on the streets of Karachi.

 Fatema and her family visited Mazar-e-Quaid, Jinnah Mausoleum; Jinnah was the founder of Pakistan. They went to Clifton beach to cool down from the intense heat in Karachi and visited Fashion Bazaar on Tariq Road for shopping. During their stay in Pakistan, they also travelled to the capital city Islamabad, followed by their visit to Lahore and Murree. The weather was cooler in these cities compared to Karachi. Islamabad, the capital city of Pakistan, is beautiful. They went sightseeing and visited Faisal Mosque, a beautiful structure. In the city of Lahore, they visited the Sheesh Mahal – the 'palace of mirrors,' – and the Lahore Fort. They also visited a marketplace where they bought cricket bat and gear for Arif. Murree's weather was very cold and frosty; they visited beautiful churches there and also went on the Patriyata chair lift. They then visited the Kashmir Point, a major attraction in Murree.

***

Amana graduated from her university and got a job for a year as a trainee and thereafter, as a dentist and a general practitioner. She is now working as a dentist/orthodontist in Worcestershire and also in Birmingham. Amana lives in a five-bedroom barn converted house and drives a Porsche car. She had a Muslim wedding, Nikah, and a reception for Muslim friends that took place at Mughal-e-Azam restaurant. She also had a second reception at Safari Lodge reception Hall that was full of entertainment. There was a spectacular display of fireworks, a magician, and many other entertaining activities like stick-dancing, which is common in Asian culture.

Amana is a very attractive girl. As traditional and cultural practice, many suitors with their parents visited her at home; this usually happens when the girl is over 17. Amana was only 15 – too young when the suiters started visiting their home. She wanted to finish her education and was not ready for marriage. The suitors continued visiting her until she was in her mid-thirties when she told her mum that the suitors did not 'tick' her 'boxes' and that she was old enough to 'find' her own match via the internet on community websites. The same was the case with Fatema's second daughter, Tahera, and her son Arif. Many suitors with good qualifications contacted them, but none were suitable. Mum Fatema was worried and tried to 'find' partners to introduce to them; she put their names down in the mosque's matrimonial committee.

Traditionally, the father takes responsibility for 'finding' a suitable partner for his children, but Shiraz took no interest in Fatema's children's welfare; he refused when Fatema asked him.

***

Fatema's sister Sukayna and her family lived in Montreal in Canada. Fatema with her family visited them; they went sightseeing in Montreal and travelled to Toronto in a coach, going to see the Niagara Falls that is one of the most famous waterfalls in the world. This magnificent waterfall is nature's creation and not man-made. It is a group of 3 waterfalls on the Niagara River, which flows from Lake Erie to Lake Ontario.

They also went on The Maid of the Mist boat tour; they were given waterproof hooded jackets, but they were soaked, drenched to the skin, with the spray mist from the waterfalls. The boat went remarkably close to the falls.

They visited New York City and saw the World Trade Centre (the twin towers) from a distance. Just nearby, there were traders selling cheap designer clothes, t-shirts, and jeans. Fatema's children bought a few clothes from there.

They also visited the Statue of Liberty. The statue is a representation of the Roman goddess, Libertas; it is a symbol of liberty, justice, and democracy and is a breath-taking, gigantic structure and a living history; 'Liberty Enlightening the World,' was a gift of friendship from the people of France to the people of the United States to mark the two countries' alliance during the American Revolution and was dedicated on 28 October 1886, designated as a National Monument in 1924.

Once inside, in the pedestal/foot of the statue, they explored the museum and bought a souvenir from the gift shop. They then climbed up 354 steps from the pedestal to the crown platform (equivalent to 20 stories) and back. There is no elevator access from the statue's feet to the statue's head.

Fatema, like all Muslims, wanted to go to Hajj when her children were older. Amana was eighteen and was awaiting her A-level results. Fatema's youngest brother Galeb and his wife Marzia were planning to go to Hajj the year Amana was studying, preparing for her A-level exams. They asked Fatema to join them; Fatema said Amana was taking her exams and would go next year, so Galeb decided to postpone the trip and wait for her. A year later, the same trip was organised by their community, so they arranged to join the group from the mosque. Fatema had saved up for it.

Shiraz being jealous did not want Fatema to go to the holy place. Behind Fatema's back, he phoned all his siblings, telling them, "She's going to perform Hajj; a woman is not allowed to go there on her own without her husband." Fatema thought, *what husband? He never was a husband.* One of Shiraz's sisters, Faiza, phoned Fatema to tell her that she cannot go and has to wait for Shiraz to go with him the following year. Fatema told her that she was going with her brother Galeb and his wife Marzia, and she might not be alive next year. Shiraz's sister said, "You can't go, and you have to listen to your husband." Fatema repeated, "I might not be alive later; do you guarantee my life?" Faiza said, "Yes, I guarantee it."

Shiraz refused to feed his family; there was no question he would never go to Hajj or anywhere with them. He was too stingy to spend his money. Ten years later, Shiraz went to Hajj with the community members after his brothers persuaded him to go, counting every penny!

There was a seminar in the mosque to explain all the rituals of performing Hajj. Galeb, his wife, and Fatema attended the seminar. A taxi from Birmingham to Heathrow was organised by the community. There were three doctors, nurses, and medical professionals, who were volunteers in the Hajj group. The flight was from Heathrow to Jeddah, where the group stayed overnight. That night, Fatema sighted the new moon and calculated Hajj Day would be Friday (it is known that if the day of Hajj falls on a Friday, it is called Akbari Hajj, which is equivalent to forty Hajj). Jedda mosque was the most beautiful structure Fatema had ever seen. She and the group that she was travelling with prayed in the mosque.

Hajj was the most wonderful experience ever! From Jedda to Madinah, Fatema saw and prayed in beautiful mosques, and after that, the group travelled to Mecca, where the stunning and the world's largest mosque Masjid al-

Haram stands. The religious building at the heart of Saudi Arabia's pilgrimage site, that covers 356,800 square meters with a capacity of 4,000,000 people. When Fatema first sighted the black stone, the Holy Kaaba, it felt magical. She was advised to make three wishes, saying, "When you see the Kaaba for the first time; all your wishes will be fulfilled." Fatema made her three wishes she wished for her three children's long, healthy, happy, contented life. She wished for world peace and to eradicate hunger, poverty, and racism that she had experienced and suffered at her work. And her third wish was for all who had asked Fatema to pray for their wishes to be granted. She knew and believed that her Lord, God, is her saviour, had always been there for her, and will answer all the prayers. The trip was very well organised by the community.

For Fatema's 50th birthday, she and her three adult children went to Egypt. They went on the Nile Cruise from Luxor to Aswan and took a flight to Cairo to see one of the oldest of the seven wonders of the ancient world, The Great Pyramids of Giza and the Sphinx. They stayed in the five-star Pyramid Hotel in Cairo; they also visited Abu Simbel temples.

When Amana was forty, they all went to Dubai and Abu Dhabi on a ten-day cruise, which made for a brilliant holiday. In Dubai, they visited Burj Khalifa, which is the tallest building in the world.

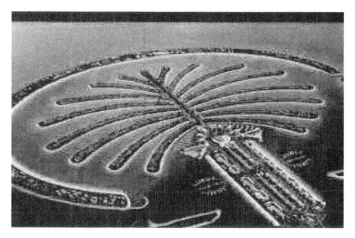

The Palm, a man-made island, viewed from above, looks like a palm tree. It is the world's first man-made built landmass and series of an artificial group of islands. One of the world's most daring developments, the Palm Jumeirah is a haven for vacationers. Jutting out into the Arabian Gulf, this man-made archipelago is lined with luxury villas and five-star hotels.

They visited the seven-star hotel Burj Al Arab Jumeirah that is suspended 657 feet above sea level where they as guests had to dress formally/smartly. They enjoyed afternoon tea and cocktails of seafood.

On Fatema's sixtieth birthday, they went to see the Taj Mahal. It was a ten-day tour to India involving The Golden Triangle that included Delhi, Agra, and Jaipur. In Delhi, they visited The Red Fort and the 15th century mosque, the first mosque built in India by the Mughal emperors. They visited Raj Palace Museum and The Jal Mahal, also called Lake Palace, in the pink city of Jaipur. It was a brilliant experience. They then travelled to the city of Agra to see the Taj Mahal. The local people were friendly, helpful, and tolerant. Tourism contributes towards growth and development of a country.

The Taj Mahal, translated as 'The Crown Palace,' is an ivory-white marble mausoleum on the southern bank of the river Yamuna in the city of Agra in India. It is a monument built by Shah Jahan, a Mughal emperor, as a symbol of the love of a husband for his favourite wife, Mumtaz. It was commissioned in 1632 by the Mughal emperor who reigned from 1628 to 1658; The Taj Mahal was built to house the tomb of Mumtaz. Shah Jahan himself wanted to build the same in black for himself on the opposite side of River Yamuna, but he did not get it completed because of the cost. The Taj Mahal is the centrepiece of the 42-acre complex that includes a mosque and a guest house set in formal gardens. It is the jewel of Muslim art and one of the universally admired masterpieces of the world's heritage. Its white marble turns peachy pink at sunset and looks breathtakingly beautiful. Fatema and her daughter Tahera visited the Taj at sunset. The Taj Mahal complex is believed to have been completed in its entirety in 1653 at a cost estimated at the time to be around 32 million rupees.

Fatema and her three children went on holidays whenever they had the opportunity and if they were affordable/reasonably priced. They went to Leon, Paris, Tunisia, Marrakech, Lanzarote, Gran Canarias, Marmaris in Turkey, Istanbul, Dubai with Abu Dhabi cruise, European cruise, Uganda, and finally to Dar-e-Salaam.

Chapter 10

Fatema's full-time job with PCT was clerical work and the title was 'data information clerk'. She was the only Asian in the office of 20 and had excellent computer skills. She was constantly asked to train the managers; she did this at first but decided that she was not employed to train anyone. Her job description, like all her colleagues was that of a data clerk. She applied for a promotion but instead, the managers tried to remove her from work. Her workload increased, but she was a fast worker and managed to do all the tasks. She compared her workload with other girls in the office and decided to write to the head office. The manager at the head office called her to tell her that her presence was not welcome and that she was 'to leave.' They offered her a redundancy package, and she was told that she would receive a letter to tell her of this. No letter arrived.

The next day when she returned to work, the manager told her, "Why don't you go back to your own country?" The whole office was witness to this but told Fatema, "We will not support you." Just because she was an Asian and was applying for a higher position, no one wanted to support her; instead, they were abusive and nasty to her, to the extent that she felt scared that they might push her down the stairs or harm her. One girl was abusive, calling her 'ugly face', but Fatema ignored her. She knew they were all in her support;

when you can't fight them, you can't join or support them, but she stood her guts. The colour of her skin was not her fault, nor was her appearance; God is the creator, and she always turned to Him for guidance.

Fatema spoke to the chairman of PCT, Dr Karim, who was also president of the Muslim community of her own sect. He advised her to ignore the issue and get on with her work. He asked her to forget about anyone supporting her. Bullying and workload increased. Fatema visited the CAB (Citizens Advice Bureau) who represented Fatema in one of the meetings with the managers. CAB advised her to contact CRE (Commission for Racial Equality). She wrote several letters and had meetings with them, and they finally advised her to file the matter to court. CRE helped her lodge a court complaint. Just before the court date, they wrote to Fatema explaining that CRE funds were not available and therefore, she would have to represent herself in court. CRE said that the judge will help her and that she must get to court. In Fatema's first hearing, she was on her own, uncertain of the procedures. The defendant on the other side had their own lawyers, a barrister, and over 50 witnesses to support their defence. The case went on for a week; more witnesses came and Fatema lost her case.

Fatema got home exhausted and devastated. She prayed extremely hard and asked Lord why when there was evidence of a massive file of letters and tape recordings of meetings that Fatema had insisted to have all meetings recorded. Why did she lose her case.

Fatema remembers reading a bible story/parable. It was during the time of prophets there was a man Hassan who travelled from Medina to Iraq on his beautiful, strong stallion. When he got to his destination, a man Sadiq came over to him and said, "This is my horse; you stole it when I fell off her during the war."

Hassan said, "It's not a female horse, a mare. It's a male horse, a stallion." Hassan was a traveller and was on his own, he continued explaining that he bought the horse from a market in his own town, but Sadiq insisted that it was a mare (female) horse. Sadiq had over 50 friends from his own town who supported him. The matter got heated and it was filed to the court. The judge said if 50 witnesses are saying that it is 'she' horse, then it is a 'she' horse! That is how the case concluded. Hassan lost his stallion and did not know how to get back home. He prayed, and a friend named Ali from his own town, who was also a trader, came to Iraq and gave him his horse. Together they travelled and stayed good friends, eventually becoming successful fellow traders and business partners.

What happened in Fatema's case was similar to the case of the stallion. Fatema had no witnesses and was on her own.

One of the managers of PCT came over and told Fatema that rather than returning to work, she would have to go on a sick leave. He gave her a SSP (Statutory Sick Pay) Form and asked her to fill it up. He also advised her to see her doctor. Fatema said she was not ill/sick, but he insisted that she filled-up the form. Fatema phoned her work regarding her return to work; she had a mortgage to pay and feed her family. She was advised that she will be paid in full and that she should continue being on sick leave and visit her GP. She was required to send doctor's sick notes regularly. She visited her GP and told him that she was not ill, but her work had insisted she sent a sick note. GP wrote a sick note for a further one month.

This went on for ten more months, and finally, when she was to return to work, she was to go to a different branch of PCT and she was given a data quality job, training new staff and doing other jobs. She was told that there was nothing else for her to do. It was the same issue again. She spoke to the manager, Sue, who advised her that she could continue sick leave on full pay. The task she was given was quite easy, and it did not require much time or effort, though. Fatema had a lot of time where she had nothing to do. Her manager told her that if she were to take on a higher position, she would have to complete the ECDL (European Computer Driving Licence). This was the requirement of all staff employed in PCT regardless of their status.

Sue continued saying that she herself was doing the course. "You would have to travel to Hagley Road PCT where the trainers will prepare you for the tests," she said. Fatema asked if the test was difficult, Sue said she had not taken the test yet as a tutor had to prepare her for the test. Sue further said, "It is a three-year course. It is all done on computers; and you have to be fast and accurate. The passing marks are 85% and over; if you get below that, you will have to repeat the test. You have three chances to redo each exam."

Fatema travelled to Hagley Road to enrol in the course; the tutor escorted her to a large room full of computers and lots of students. She said Fatema would have to come every Wednesday from 9 am to 4 pm. Her first day was easy as she was computer literate; she was using her son Arif's computer at home and had a fair knowledge of it. Arif had an ECDL certificate, who showed her some of the skills. Fatema asked the tutor if she could practice on test papers ratherm than learn the lessons. She practised on the test papers for a month until she got 100% results in all the practice test papers. She was ready; it required speed and accuracy.

A student sitting next to Fatema put his hand up to ask for help from the tutor, but the tutor was busy with other students, so Fatema helped him. He said the way you explained to me is better to grasp. Fatema helped other students. The teacher seemed to be happy with her help. Because computers at the time were a new commodity, and all the medical records were transferred onto the computers, people were unfamiliar and even reluctant to use them.

Fatema did one test after another; each test an hour long, in various technology subjects: Information and Technology, using computers and managing files, word processing, spreadsheets, database, information and communication. She was allowed two exams per day, she achieved over 90% in all the tests. When she was doing her final test, the computer crashed. Fatema told the tutor, who said someone would come over to sort the problem. It crashed three times, and she was advised to return the next day to complete the final exam. The next day when she returned to work, one of the students who was close to Fatema told her that the crash was deliberate and that "they do not want you to finish your last test." Successful completion of the final test meant that she would be the first to complete a full ECDL certificate. Fatema prayed, and the next day, with a small prayer book in her possession, she went an hour early to the test centre without telling anyone. She switched on the computer, put the prayer book near it, and recited a prayer. She was able to complete the last test. She passed all the tests and received the ECDL certificate, but her work situation did not change.

A solicitor and barrister that Fatema saw cost her a lot of money. He advised her that the fact that this issue was in court before, her company would not want it to go to court again and will offer her a lump sum. He advised Fatema, who was sixty-three at the time, to take the money and leave. Fatema's grandson was born, and her daughter wanted Fatema to babysit. She took the solicitor's advice and retired, entitling herself to a private pension. Although Fatema had lost her court case in the first instance, financially, she gained more. She was better off as not only did she get one-year sick pay, but also got full pay for a further three years when she returned to work after the court case. She also got a pension lump sum at retirement. Fatema invested the money in properties and thanked God for His help.

Chapter 11

Tahera, the second daughter, whilst she was at college and university, also had weekend/holiday jobs. She went to Greenwich University in London, and after completing her master's degree, she got a job as head of a teaching association. She bought a place of her own. Tahera found her partner and came home to introduce him as James. Her dad, Shiraz, refused to see him and has never met him. An engagement party for them was held at Sister Amana's house. A few months later, the wedding took place at Monkey Island in London. Tahera invited Shiraz to the wedding in the hopes that he would send a wedding gift, but he neither attended nor sent any wedding gift. A year later, Fatema's first grandchild was born ten weeks premature; he was the size of his dad's palm and was in intensive care for two months.

Fatema travelled to London just in time to whisper Lord's prayer into the child's ears, and there after, she visited baby Adam every Sunday with Amana. Tahera had maternity leave and a year out from her work to look after the new-born. Fatema retired from work to babysit Adam and travelled to and from London every week for nearly two years until Adam was nearly three and Tahera enrolled him in a private nursery.

Adam is now eleven; Shiraz has never met/seen him or sent anything for him; his one and only grandson. He has never considered Fatema's children as his family; he says, "You had them, you feed them." He neither provided for the children nor helped with their upbringing or their education through university studies. Fatema believes that with the help of her belief, she did everything. Shiraz lives in a house he does not pay for; he refuses to pay the mortgage/rent or insurance or even food or for anything. He doesn't and has never helped with house chores and gets abusive and violent when asked for any kind of help. Shiraz steals food, biscuits, chocolates, or even cooked food that Fatema buys/cooks for her family. When Fatema tells him not to take her food that is for her family and herself, he swears, saying, "F*** your mother in her grave." Shiraz continues to steal right under her nose. He tries to hoodwink her by lying and saying Arif has taken it.

Fatema eventually decided to get away from Shiraz; he agreed to buy her out with the money that was in the joint account that Fatema did not have access to. Fatema thought if he agreed to buy her out and pay 50% of the house, she would get the house valued. She painted the dining and living room Shiraz said he would scribble all over it. Fatema called the estate agents to value the house; they advised that they could not value it until it was "cleaned out." Shipways Estate agent who valued the property, could not market the

132

house in the condition that it was until it was cleaned out. They suggested hiring a skip.

Fatema looked for a three-bedroom house that she would move into with Arif and Amana; she found one nearby. Shiraz had agreed that he would give her 50% value of the house but refused to transfer the money. Fatema told her son to ask him to transfer the money, but Shiraz said nothing. When none of the children were around, Shiraz said to Fatema he would never give her a penny. He said the house was his, and he will never move out; he made a gesture to attack her, saying, "I'll kill you." Shiraz did make several attempts to kill her.

Shiraz has a habit of collecting junk that people throw away. He collects empty tins of chocolate, empty food tubs, newspapers, broken things like toasters, printers, kettles, teapots, and old computers, TVs etc., that other people threw away. This is because he believes he could have them repaired for a few pounds and reuse them.

Hoarding is a mental health disorder where someone acquires an excessive number of items and stores them in a chaotic manner, usually resulting in unmanageable amounts of clutter. The items can be of little or no monetary value. Shiraz matches the description of a hoarder.

Shiraz hit Fatema repeatedly because he thought she was throwing away some of the old newspapers that he collects;

133

she had not. Her son Arif called the police and told them that he had witnessed the beating. The police letter regarding this incident was stolen from her room and destroyed by Shiraz.

Again, he hit her when Fatema was taking her old computers, wires, and old printers to a charity shop. "Leave my things alone!" Shiraz snatched the bags from her hands and pushed her; she fell against the table, and as she got up, he hit her so hard that she fell again, and he continued hitting her like a rag doll. She suffered broken ribs. A report from Solihull Hospital can be obtained to confirm this. Shiraz always threatened to commit suicide to his family and blamed it on Fatema, saying she was a madwoman who wanted money and was after other men.

Fatema was not aware of the things he said about her until Arif asked her, "Are you going to remarry someone?" Fatema, shocked, responded, "I am too old, and no, I am not!" When Fatema asked him what other man and who he was, Shiraz said, "Who would have this madwoman? She's divorcing me; I am so good." Fatema said, "You are too good. I am a madwoman. Go find a good woman to do your washing and ironing and providing food, paying the mortgage, and everything free of charge." He responded in swear words and again said, "F*** your mother." He added, "Go stay in her grave and f*** her 100 times," followed by a laugh.

On one occasion, when Fatema was in the shower, Shiraz turned off the hot water from the boiler. He said that she had not paid bills, Fatema had to give him a cheque for gas/electricity. On another occasion, when she was watching a TV program, Shiraz told her to get off and did not allow her to watch anything as she had to pay for the programmes. She bought heaters that cost 1p per hour to run. He pulled the socket off and would not allow it to be used unless she paid him more money. The house was never warm, but he did not allow any kind of heating on. He just warmed up his own room and sat there all day watching TV.

Another incident happened when Fatema enquired about the sugar contents of the milkshake that Arif was having. Shiraz hit her so hard that her hand was all bruised and swollen. It was very painful. The doctor confirmed that she had a hairline fracture. She had to take painkillers. He constantly swears and is abusive and violent. He was harassing her family and lied to the police to get Arif arrested twice. He said Arif hit him and also lied to the doctors, saying Arif was stressed because his mother was divorcing such a good husband that he is. He believes he's good looking and constantly stands in front of the mirror grooming and admiring himself. To his relatives, to the whole world of his, he said he was a good husband and father, and Fatema was a madwoman.

Fatema's son Arif passed GCSE and IB (International Baccalaureate Diploma) with high grades. His results were equivalent to both his sisters added together. Mum's home tuition and prayers helped all three children pass successfully. Thereafter, Arif went to Leicester University to study Law with French. He went to University De Leon to study, which was funded by his university. Fatema and Amana visited the university as Arif requested them to go during the summer holidays when the students' accommodation was vacant. During the August holidays, they both stayed in the students' halls/accommodation for a week. Arif took them sightseeing; he was a great host. Leon is a beautiful city, and his university was great. They travelled by train to Geneva in Switzerland to see the Geneva Conventions building; they had a guided tour to see inside where the world's presidents sat to discuss weapon deals. The total number of States Party was 196.

In 1949, following the horrors of the second world war, world leaders gathered in Switzerland to sign the Geneva Conventions. All 196 countries ratified the international treaty that established the standards of international law for humanitarian treatment in war. The singular term Geneva Convention usually denotes the agreements of 1949, negotiated in the aftermath of the Second World War (1939–1945), which updated the terms of the two 1929 treaties, and added two new conventions. The Geneva Conventions extensively defined the basic rights of wartime prisoners (civilians and military personnel), established protections for the wounded and sick, and established protections for the civilians in and around a war zone. The treaties of 1949 were endorsed; the Geneva Convention also defines the rights and protections to non-combatants. The Geneva Conventions are about soldiers in war; they do not address the use of weapons of war, which are the subject of the Hague Conventions and the bio-chemical warfare, Geneva Protocol.

Fatema was interested in this subject as she introduced the British Red Cross Society at her school. The International Red Cross and Red Crescent Movement started in 1863 and was inspired by Swiss businessman Henry Dunant. He reversed the Swiss Flag that was a white cross on a red background to a red cross on white background.

The suffering of thousands of men on both sides of the Battle upset Dunant. Many were left to die due to lack of care. He proposed creating national relief societies made up of volunteers trained in peacetime to provide neutral and impartial help to relieve suffering in times of war. In response to these ideas, a committee that later became the International Committee of the Red Cross was established in Geneva. The founding charter of the Red Cross was drawn up in 1863. Dunant also proposed that countries adopt an international agreement, which would recognise the status of medical services and of the wounded on the battlefield. This agreement – the original Geneva Convention – was adopted in 1864.

The Formation of the British Red Cross

When war broke out between France and Prussia in July 1870, Colonel Loyd-Lindsay called for a National Society to be formed in Britain just like in other European nations. a National Society be formed in this country for aiding sick and wounded soldiers in times of war and that the said Society be formed upon the rules laid down by the Geneva Convention of 1864. On 4 August 1870, a public meeting was held in London, and a resolution passed.

After a year at Universite De Lyon, Arif went back to London University to complete the final year in Law. He was unable to secure a training contract in a law firm; at the time, he encountered racism. He had a lot of interviews but had no luck. He did voluntary work at a local CAB (Citizens Advice Bureau), he worked in schools and various other places. The Job Centre said to him that his qualifications were too high. "Our authority (British) has failed you," were his words. Arif was extremely intellectual but was experiencing racism; that was the problem. He worked part-time in a local supermarket so he could pay for part-time LPC Legal Practice Course further studies in Law.

Fatema and her children went on holidays; they never write Shiraz (husband/father) as 'next of kin' on their passports; in schools, universities, or at work. They always put down the mother's name and contact numbers/details as a 'next of kin,' and Fatema, to date, puts her daughter's and son's names and contact details on her passport. This made Shiraz very jealous and hostile; he believes that Arif being a male should write his father's name as his 'next of kin' and the girls should put mother's name. He said, "I'll show you who his next of kin is," and started swearing using B*** and F***, bad-mouthing Fatema, and beating/hitting her. He also started stealing all their passports etc., one thing at a time and then lied to the children that mum took them. Shiraz also stole Arif's credit cards, his car keys, house keys, glasses, important documents, and many other important things that Arif needed and blamed it on Fatema.

Shiraz held the holy book in his hand and swore by the Quran that he had not taken them. Arif searched for his missing items high and low but in vain. He used spare car keys and borrowed Fatema's credit card/password for fuel in his car. Fatema pleaded to Shiraz, saying, "Why are you doing this? Arif's driving without his glasses. He needs his credit cards... poor man. Don't you feel sorry for him?"

Shiraz kept quiet. After four to five days, he put each item back, saying, "I only touched English Quran, not the Arabic one." Shiraz laughed and said to Fatema, "Arif hates you; he thinks you are stealing his things. Even Amana thinks you've stolen all the things." Fatema pleaded to Amana that her own things were missing too, all her bank/insurance documents, passport, her prayer books/beads.

Shiraz continued stealing food, biscuits, chocolates; he was stealing everything right under Fatema's nose and said that Fatema told him to "Put the chocolates back. They are for my children." Shiraz started swearing, "F*** your mother, f*** your sisters."

When Fatema told her adult children the truth, they did not want to know, so Fatema raised her hands and prayed aloud. "May Allah cut off the hand of the one who steals, and the tongue of the one who lies!" Fatema continued to quote, "Even if you paid me thousands of pounds, I would not steal or lie; it is sin/haram." We're not only to avoid lying ourselves, we're also to avoid supporting liars in their sin.

And do not argue on behalf of those who deceive themselves. Indeed, Allah loves not one who is a habitually sinful deceiver. [Quran, 4:107]

We don't need to worry about guarding ourselves against deception; Allah is ever ready to protect us.

140

Indeed, Allah does not guide one who is a transgressor and a liar.' [Quran, 40:28]

Lord, please protect the innocent victims from the one who lies. (16:92).

Fatema knows Almighty God would always help her although her children are now growing up hating her as Shiraz continues to bad-mouth her.

Chapter 12

In 2010, Fatema petitioned for divorce; she could not take the pain and suffering anymore. She had been a single mother all her life; they were not living together for over 25 years. Shiraz panicked when he received the divorce papers. He thought divorce meant the money in the joint account that amounted over £500,000 would have to be split and the house would go too. So, he first tried sweet-talking. "Please, I don't want to divorce you; I will refuse to sign the papers." When Fatema stuck to her point, told him he will have to sign the papers or go to prison, Shiraz decided to murder Fatema, who always wore a *ta'wiz* (Amulet) to protect herself. He made a few attempts but failed. He said, "You think your *ta'wiz* will protect you? He thumped her and swore, "F*** your mother in her grave; do it 100 times and stay there." He told Arif that his mum was a madwoman and she dressed nice when going out to attract men. He said all Fatema wanted was sex, which was why she was divorcing him as he was old and could not give her enough. Shiraz also said that he was going to commit suicide and wept crocodile tears. He said if Arif, his son, helped him kill her, he would pay him £200,000. All this was happening behind Fatema's back. Her own family had no respect for Fatema.

Shiraz told all his lies to his five brothers and their families, all their relatives. He even phoned Fatima's sisters individually to tell them lies about the reason behind the divorce. Fatema's sisters and their adult children started calling her on the phone, telling her to think about her own family they were upset.

After the divorce, the house was to be cleaned out; Arif asked Fatema again if she was going to remarry. Fatema said, "No, I am too old, and I'd never remarry even if I was young." When Fatema realised something was wrong and all were against her, she gave the divorce papers to her son Arif to show him there was no 'other man' and the true reason for the divorce was:

- "Unreasonable behaviour."

- "Harassment, bullying, & beating. I suffered broken bones."

- "He never gave me a penny. I pay the mortgage, my daughter's education, her wedding. He is a miser, a stinger; he refuses to feed his own children. I was not allowed to use my own money that I was earning. I was to bring money from my parents. He refused to acknowledge his daughters."

- "He collected rubbish and ruined the house. Estate agents will not market my property."

- "He is transferring out money from the joint account and said that I would not have a penny from it."

- "He threatened to remove my name from the deeds of my home."

Fatema forwarded copies of her divorce petition papers to her sisters via emails. She did not care if they chose to believe Shiraz; he is a liar, a thief, and a criminal. She wanted him out of her house. She was going to divorce him at any cost. She had a solicitor to represent her in court.

Fatema's strong belief in Almighty God helped her, and she always thanks Him. Shiraz realised that Fatema had proof/evidence of bank statements of paying for everything. At the courts, Shiraz did not disclose his cash assets that were initially in the joint account with Fatema. He paid his solicitor a lot of money to move the lump sum from the joint account and 'hide' it by freezing the bank account. He also wanted the house that he never paid for, and he made several attempts to kill Fatema; he was prepared to pay a large amount to have her killed. He tried to poison her food and tried several other tricks. Fatema knew he would damage/sabotage her car; she was cautious and slept with her car keys in her pyjama pocket.

Shiraz told Amana that mum would not allow Arif to take medication and that Arif is suffering from severe depression and needs to take medication. Amana was furious and told him to "call the police and have mum arrested." Fatema said to Amana there's nothing wrong with Arif, he was suffering side effects from prescription drugs, but she was not prepared to listen. Shiraz contacted the police with lies to have Fatema arrested, saying she was a madwoman. Police went to Fatema's house; she told them there was nothing wrong with her, and she was not mad, they left when she said this was private property, they were not welcome. In his divorce papers, Shiraz had written via his solicitor to the court that his son was extremely ill and, being a concerned parent, he was looking after him. 'His mum cannot control him, so my son and I should live in the house as I look after him.'

This is what was written in Shiraz's divorce form:

"My son, Arif, is suffering from severe depression and schizophrenia and is being cared for by me. I would describe my standard of living as average; I have not taken a holiday in the last 12 months as I have been caring for my son."

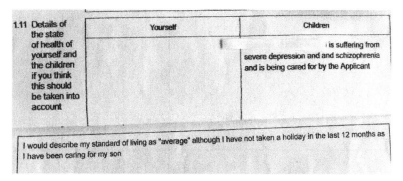

1.11 Details of the state of health of yourself and the children if you think this should be taken into account	Yourself	Children
		i is suffering from severe depression and and schizophrenia and is being cared for by the Applicant

I would describe my standard of living as "average" although I have not taken a holiday in the last 12 months as I have been caring for my son

The psychiatrist. Dr Khan wrote a letter to the GP stating:

"Arif's father called here in April to request a letter supporting that his son should live with him rather than his mother. However, we have not been able to discuss this with his son, and as an adult, he has a choice and freedom to decide this himself. We did explain this to the father. I understand he has chosen not to take medication at all. The family has not raised concerns."

father has called here in April to request a letter supporting that his son should live
M   with him rather than mother; however we have not been able to discuss this with M   and
as an adult he has choice and freedom to decide this himself. We did explain this to the father and have
asked him to encourage M   1 to re attend or make contact. I understand that he has not
chosen to have any medication at all. The family have not raised any further questions or concerns.

I am therefore unable to reassess at present and I am copying this to M   and his family by
way of information and to encourage them to please make contact. M   and his family are
aware to contact us here at Spring Road Centre on 0121 678 4050, and PALS can be contacted by calling
0800 953 0045 (Weekdays between 8am and 8pm), texting 07985 883 509 or by emailing
pals@bsmhft.nhs.uk

Thank you - yours sincerely,

Dr Geof Khan
Consultant Psychiatrist

He further continued, "He is not in any way physically hostile; I did not find him depressed. He does not describe any hallucinations."

Fatema had an interview with the psychiatrist and gave him copies of divorce papers to explain that his father wants the house and does not want to move out.

Dr Loizou, the psychiatrist, came with a health visitor, a social worker, and several police officers to assess/arrest Fatema. Shiraz told Dr Loizou, "His (Arif's) mother is not allowing Arif to take tablets; she needs to be arrested and forced out of the house."

Fatema insisted there was nothing wrong with her and that she had divorced him, not the other way round. She said she was not stressed but incredibly happy. She should have divorced him a long time ago. Dr Loizou said that Fatema was to leave her house and let her husband, Shiraz, have her house. She continued saying, "You want money, a lot of money from your husband? You are greedy. You want your head tested." Fatema told Loizou that she (the doctor) was not welcome in her house as it is private property. She asked them to leave. Shiraz said he had 50% ownership of the house and had invited them, but Fatema insisted for them to leave as Shiraz was not her husband nor the owner of her home. He could not prove it. The doctor left but Fatema received a letter from Loizou saying that Fatema needed treatment and must see her doctor immediately.

Shiraz was planning Fatema to be admitted into a psychiatric hospital; he contacted his GP and told him, "She's a madwoman."

GP phoned Fatema to inform her that an appointment had been booked for her. Fatema was confused but saw the GP, who told her that she was suffering from severe depression/stress. "Your husband had informed me," he said. When Fatema told the GP that Shiraz was the one suffering because he had attempted to kill her, the GP said that Dr Loizou had assessed her and had advised her GP to prescribe drugs for her. Fatema always had a strong belief in her religion; she wears her *ta'wiz* (the amulet that contains verses from Quran, the holy book) and believes that it has protected her from the torment that Arif was suffering.

present at the time of this assessment which was not relevant at the present time. or not he attends a psychiatrist under the care of BUPA is not relevant at the present time. However, if you wish your son to receive psychiatric care whilst detained under Section 3 in a private psychiatric hospital you could advise his current treating psychiatrist, Dr Singsit Evans who will need to know who the treating psychiatrist would be, at which hospital they are based and arrangements could potentially be made for his transfer of care to a private psychiatric hospital bed under Section 3. However this may of course incur a significant financial cost to yourselves.

You will recall that at the time of us assessing your son on the 16th, the attending police officer advised you that you yourself needed to seek medical attention as he felt you were mentally unwell. This was also the opinion of the psychiatric team who were present that day. You did say that you would go and see your general practitioner to get medical help for yourself and I hope you will do this. You did also say that you would no longer discourage Muhammad from taking medication and from keeping his appointments, stating that you would not interfere with his psychiatric treatment in the future - we all commended you upon this. Hence I was disappointed to have received your letter.

You will recall that the Warstock Lane team were notified by the police of Muhammad's arrest earlier in the month and this, in combination with the fact that he had failed to attend his outpatient appointment with me and had stopped taking his psychiatric medication, subsequently is the reason that we had to perform the mental health act assessment at home. Fortunately we were able to gain access without requiring a police warrant on this occasion.

I will pass a copy of this letter to Dr Singsit Evans at the Oleaster.

Yours sincerely,

Dr E Loizou
Consultant Psychiatrist

Cc   Dr Singsit Evans

Dr Loizou had written to Fatema saying, "At the time of assessing your son, we thought that you yourself needed to seek medical attention as the doctor felt you were mentally unwell. This was the opinion of the psychiatric team." Fatema thought about who would help Arif if she was locked up and forced to take drugs in a psychiatric hospital.

Fatema knew Loizou being a psychiatrist had the power to force her; fortunately, she was divorced and had papers to prove it, so Shiraz was not her nearest relative. She showed her passport to Loizou to show her that she never had Shiraz's name in her passport. "My next of kin is my son, and there is absolutely nothing wrong with either of us. Shiraz is the one who is stressed and needs treatment." Fatema also told her that she was paying the mortgage. Shiraz said, "She's lying." Fortunately, Arif supported his mum and the team left.

Adam, Fatema's grandson, was one, and Tahera's year out was ending, she therefore wanted mum to babysit for her. Whilst Fatema was travelling to and from London, babysitting Adam, Arif was not eating well, although Fatema had cooked a lot of food and put it in the freezer. She told Arif that food in the freezer was for him. Unfortunately, Shiraz convinced Arif that he was suffering from depression and needed to see a psychiatrist. He said he would get free prescription drugs.

Shiraz told the doctors that Arif, who was now in his thirties, was suffering from depression. He said Arif talked to himself and convinced the doctor with all lies to get free medication and treatment. Shiraz believed medication is good for us even when we do not need it. The doctor sent a letter to Arif and arranged an appointment saying his father was worried and needed to see him for a check-up. Arif saw his GP, who then refered him to a psychiatrist Dr Loizou.

After several interviews and counselling with Dr Loizou, Arif spoke with Dr Khan, a senior consultant. With Shiraz present in all interviews and counselling, putting his own words in his mouth and forcing Arif to admit that he required treatment. Loizou told Arif that it would be a very small dose of one mg tablets that would be discontinued after a short period of time. Fatema was not aware of this issue as she was busy babysitting and travelling to and from London. When Arif started acting differently, he seemed to be very obedient. Following his father's instructions, she asked if he was OK. He was aggressive, rude, and nasty to Fatema. He had not been eating well, the food in the freezer was not eaten, Arif was hangry; he had not eaten well for days. She asked Arif why he hadn't eaten or taken his sandwiches to work. He said he did not know they were for him, and that his dad Shiraz told him he was to buy his own food. He hadn't been eating at all.

Shiraz said, "I got some free tablets from the doctors for Arif." Fatema was alarmed; she said, "What's wrong with him? Why does he need tablets?" Arif was weak, hungry, and lethargic; he was sleeping all the time and was taking psychotic tablets behind her back. She took the tablets and checked online to see what they were for and what were the side effects of the tablets. The side effects showed that the patient gets a high appetite, remains hungry, gains pounds and muscle tremor, gets depressed, is suicidal, etc.

Fatema was shocked! "Are you trying to kill my son?" she yelled. "He does not need tablets; he needs food." Shiraz said he had to buy his own food. "I am not giving him mine. Not even a piece of bread."

Fatema asked, "Why was he not allowed to eat from the freezer? That's not your food. Those free tablets are prescription drugs and are dangerous!" She followed online instructions tried to reduce his dose to half a tablet for one week and have half every other day the following week until he stopped taking them gradually. But behind her back, whilst she was in London babysitting, Shiraz forced him to take more tablets. Shiraz told the psychiatrist that his mother, the madwoman, will not allow him to take medication and arranged for a regular home visit by a nurse to monitor his medication. Shiraz had control over Arif's mind, making him feel low about himself and saying he was not good enough as he did not have a job like his sisters who all had well-paid jobs, and that no one would marry him, etc.

Arif trying hard to please his father even took a higher dose prescribed by his psychiatrist. His dose was increasing every few months and got to 10mg. Fatema could not do anything about it; she advised him to pretend to take it but spit it out in the toilet. Shiraz found out that he was flushing the tablets; he told the psychiatrist who changed the tablets to give him depo-injections instead. When Arif refused to take the injections, Dr Loizou sent five huge men who held Arif down and forced an injection in his back. This continued once a week for a while he was forced to take a small dose of 5mg depo injections. Arif said, "Mum, leave it, I can take it. There's nothing we can do." Arif was putting on weight; his mind was not functioning. No matter how small the dose of psychotic drugs was, the effect was obvious.

The side effects were horrendous. He was shaking and had muscle tremor/spasm. His whole body was shaking like in Parkinson's, and he wanted to die. He told Fatema he was fed up and wanted to die. Fatema wept and did not know what to do. She prayed hard, asking for Almighty's help; she got up half an hour before morning prayers to pray extra prayers called 'Shab' for forty days. She had faith in God's favourable response.

Fatema's babysitting, which was three or four days a week, seized as Tahera wanted Adam to go to a private nursery near her workplace.

Once again, Shiraz told Dr Loizou what he had told his GP – that his son Arif was stressed, self-talked, and was suicidal. Dr Loizou assessed him and said he would have to go to the hospital to be investigated. Arif refused to go; he said he was not well, that he had tonsillitis and had to go to work in the morning. Arif locked himself in his bedroom. Shiraz insisted that being his 'nearest relative' and as the oldest person in the family, he had taken this action, and Arif must go with the police. Arif refused to open the door, so the police broke the door open. As a result, Arif opened the window and jumped onto the roof. Fatema shouted and warned him that the police had a gun, and they would shoot. Arif pulled out a roof tile to shield himself; he held the tile on his chest.

Fatema put herself in front of the gun and said, "You have to shoot me first; I'll not let you harm my son." She said to Shiraz, "Why are you doing this? You want the house?"

Shiraz said, "I want you to die."

Fatema said, "You can have the money and the house. Please leave him alone."

Shiraz had called the police to arrest Fatema, but somehow Arif became his victim. Police tasered him to immobilise him. The taser dart lodged near his stomach. Fatema asked Arif if it hurt; Arif nodded his head to indicate that it was painful. Police handcuffed him and took him to the hospital to have the taser dart removed, then took him to the police station and locked him up in a cell. Shiraz jumping with joy, phoned his brothers to tell them how clever he was to get Arif free accommodation and free drugs; he said, "They will keep him in for six months!"

Fatema, worried, went online to check some facts about taser guns and found that if hit in the chest, it could lead to cardiac arrest and sudden death. Fatema was worried that Arif had not eaten and was not well. She prayed all night; she could not sleep. The next day in the afternoon, Arif phoned, "Mum, pick me up!" and gave the address of the police station. Fatema picked him up, Arif was not well so he slept in the back seat. When they got home, Arif went upstairs, took Penicillin, an antibiotic prescribed by his GP for tonsilitis. His mum gave him some lemonade. He felt a bit better after a few hours' sleep. Fatema then made chicken soup for him. She sat down with him, wanting to know everything.

Arif said at the police station, he was taken in an empty room and asked to look around. He said he was asked, "How many people can you see in the room?" Arif answered, "Just you and me."

"Look carefully again," they said and Arif said, "And God."

"Can you see God?" the other man asked.

"No," Arif replied.

People suffering from schizophrenia usually see invisible beings/people and hear voices. This starts in early childhood. Arif had never suffered any physical or mental illness, though. He was a top student highly intellectual.

A Beautiful Mind is a 2001 biographical drama film based on the life of the American mathematician John Nash, a Nobel Laureate in Economics and Abel Prize winner who suffered from schizophrenia. Nash could see and talk to people no one else could see them. A human drama inspired by events based on the biography of John Forbes, Nash Jr. experienced paranoia and delusions. A mathematical genius, he made an astonishing discovery early in his career and stood on the brink of international acclaim.

Arif never suffered from any such delusions. In prison, he was not given any food. This is what happens: they make the victim starve, so they become hangry and behave badly enough for them to have an excuse to lock them up. Arif had not done anything wrong; he could not see any invisible being. He was released -they let him go.

Fatema told Arif that she would not allow anyone to enter her house, that the house was hers unless Shiraz could prove it otherwise. Shiraz had no paperwork to prove anything. Fatema always dealt with the mortgage and kept all the papers.

Arif was ill because of the side effects of drugs, but Shiraz has a weird mentality. He thinks that all medications are for a cure only and cannot harm anyone. He told Amana that their mum would not allow Arif to take medication that would make him better. "She is a madwoman," he said. Amana told him to call the police and have her mum arrested. Once again, Fatema told Amana there was nothing wrong with Arif and the drugs were causing side effects. Shiraz called the police, who came, but Arif was not in; he was shopping with his mum. Fatema took him everywhere she went; she was too scared to leave him on his own as she knew the police would restrain and arrest him, for they would always obey Shiraz as he has white skin.

Shiraz was also very deceitful; he fooled everyone by saying that Fatema was a madwoman seeking male attention. Arif was also fooled by dad Shiraz's crocodile tears, saying he was old and unable to give her attention. Fatema was unaware of the situation but noticed that Arif was distancing himself from her.

Fatema told Shiraz to leave her son alone and told him that he was tarnishing his son Arif's medical records, making employment difficult. "University will not admit him. His medical records show the mental health treatment he is receiving," Fatema told Amana and even Arif, but they did not listen to her. Fatema told her God that He was her saviour that she knew her silent prayers would be answered. Almighty had always been with her since childhood. Shiraz had ruined her son's career, his marriage prospects, and his life. Arif was trying to find a partner and get married, so Fatema told Arif to pray; she put prayer books in his room, prayed silently, and cried a lot. Arif was a good person; he had worked hard all through his education and got good grades throughout. He also worked. He had done nothing wrong. Why was Lord punishing him? Fatema was feeling the pain of his suffering. She suffered humiliation for producing girls, Shiraz had refused to acknowledge his family, refused to provide for them, harassed her, was rude, uttered swear words, and even beat her. However, the most painful thing was that her son was suffering, going through mental trauma, and was forced to take prescription drugs. "Oh, my Lord, please help!" Fatema begged.

Fatema told Shiraz that he could have the house for free. "You don't have to pay, just pay the mortgage and the insurance. Leave Arif alone," she said. He refused to pay and is still living free of charge. He steals food and whatever he wanted; he had always done this. Shiraz is a thief, a liar, and a criminal for he had attempted murder. But who was going to believe Fatema? Her only saviour, Almighty God, who helped her throughout her life, was her closest companion.

Shiraz tried to get what he could for free from NHS, including free medication, free treatment, and free hospitalisation. Fatema knew he was trying to milk the NHS as much as he could. Arif was receiving treatment of depo/injections. Shiraz said each injection cost £160. He smiled, satisfied. Fatema knew her son Arif is the best person in the world and had low self-esteem because of the situation he was in. He was still trying to please everyone, especially his dad, Shiraz, who told him he was useless and that no one would marry him. Arif had a big beard and long hair, was a Muslim, and had the appearance of a terrorist as per his dad. The psychiatrists were cautious of him. They believed that he heard voices, could harm someone or himself, and was involved in some criminal activity.

A person with low self-esteem has low regard for themselves, which can manifest itself in traits like indecisiveness, hypersensitivity to criticism, and guilt. Whilst low self-esteem does not make up a condition alone, it does in combination with other symptoms including anxiety, depression, bipolar disorder and personality disorders.

Dr Loizou
Warstock Lane Centre
Warstock Lane
Billesley
Birmingham
B14 4AP

Your Ref: 1029457

15 July 2014

Dear Dr Loizou

Re: CTO

Herewith please find a copy of letter from SIA – I am unable to get any job like stewarding at cricket and football matches. 30 people who paid and trained for the SIA course all (except me) have received their badges and are in employment since March 2013.

I would therefore like you to write to SIA and help me to obtain employment of any sort (not in first line). Herewith please find SIA Certificate and my CV in the hope that you will be able to find me employment. I know that I have not got schizophrenia; I would like to know why I have been diagnosed / treated for schizophrenia.

Last July 2013 in the month of fasting I nearly passed out 3 times; you agreed that this was due to the medication (injections) that I was receiving but continued to force the medication. I am fasting again this year therefore would like to get off the medication for at least 6 months.

Yours sincerely

Arif is very intellectual but unlucky. He wrote to Dr Loizou regarding the side effects of the drugs but all in vain. He wrote to his solicitor, who represented Arif in manager's meetings with a psychiatrist, social worker, and Shiraz being nearest relative was present in all meetings.

Quality Solicitors
82 High Street
Brownhills
Walsall
WS8 6EW

17 February 2015

Dear Mr Bradley

Re: Discharge from CTO

Thank you for representing me at the Manager's Review on 16 February. I would just like to say that I believe the meeting is pointless as there is no chance the panel of lay manager's will discharge the patient.

Herewith enclosed please find documents you requested, a letter from solicitor (Ref SRM/IT/3144) to the owner of the property next door. There is also a letter from Thompsons Solicitors which was written in November 2012.

The psychiatrist has stated that I am paranoid about builders next-door – I am not paranoid, I have dealt with issues with the neighbours via a solicitor. I was beaten up severely on my drive by people next door; I have hospital report. I did not want any fuss or treatment as the waiting at outpatient was so long I was tired and in pain and wanted to go home. Next day my foot and ankle were swollen; my mum said the swelling indicates that I had fractured my bones and needed treatment. I did not go to hospital again but was limping for six months.

My father is a bully, because I grew my hair long my father said I looked like a Satan (devil) and I would go to hell for not praying five times a day like he did.
I never ever hit anyone. My father said that he felt a tap on his head and thought I hit him. I assured him that I did not hit him.

My parents were going through a divorce and I was fed up of their arguments; for 40 years my mum has suffered physical and verbal abuse from my father. See Police letter attached.

I hope that I will be able to see the independent doctor during an evening or weekend. I would also like to add that I am not really benefitting from attending the appointments at the Zinnia Centre with the psychiatrist.

Yours sincerely

Chapter 13

Fatema remembers that when she was ten, her best companion was her strong belief in Almighty God. She was on her way home from school; it was evening time and some extraordinarily strong force pushed her against a concrete wall. She lay on the floor for a few minutes, got up, and rushed home very scared of Satan/Jinn, that is believed to be spirits or demons that are supernatural invisible creatures. She did not mention the incident to anyone but never walked that way again.

Fatema's friend Salma's older sister Najma, who was thirteen at the time, was possessed by a Satan/Jinn. It was very scary to see their items moving from places and dishes and plates with food turning upside down right in front of their eyes! Najma even had seizures and epileptic fits. Her family put Quran and prayer books in her room, but they witnessed pages being razor cut into pieces by an invisible being. Najma could see Satan doing the act, but no one else could. Her little sister Salma tried to intervene, but Satan slapped her across her face; there were finger marks on her face, but no one, not even Salma, could see the being who had slapped her. Everyone was afraid of the invisible Satan and were vigilant/careful. They took great precautions not to go under trees in the evenings or during prayer times. Najma was possessed by Satan because she went to pick mangoes in the evening while Satan was doing his prayers under the tree; she walked on his path unknowingly. Najma's family performed many prayers and religious rituals. They were advised by the great religious preachers and was taken to a high priest in Zanzibar to perform an exorcism.

Exorcism is the religious or spiritual practice bound by oath for eviction of demons or other spiritual entities from a person or an area that is believed to be possessed. The high priest in Zanzibar recites verses from the Quran that adjures the demon out of a person. The demon adjured out of Najma was lured into a bottle tightly closed forever. Najma said just before the jinn/devil left her, he told her he'll come back to get her. The priest told Najma's family to leave Zanzibar immediately and NEVER to return. The bottle was thrown into the far side of the ocean by the priest who travelled by boat to the middle of the ocean. He tied a heavy stone to the bottle and recited a prayer before lowering it into the ocean. Zanzibar was commonplace for performing exorcisms and religious rituals. Fatema, like all Muslims, had faith in all religious rituals.

Najma returned home to her normal life; being cautious, the family moved nearer the mosque, away from trees. Years later, the Muslim priest who had performed the exorcism was killed mysteriously. It was believed that the jinn may have returned. Everyone was cautious and avoided walking under trees in the evenings. In those days people did not fear being mugged as much as they feared the invisible jinn and devils, and most would wear *ta'wiz/* Amulet that has verses from Quran for protection.

Fatema's next-door neighbours, Usman Khan and wife Sofia Begum, were having their bungalow renovated. They demolished the entire bungalow to build a three story-five-bedroom house and approached Shiraz for a supply of electricity in return for a wall to be built between the two neighbours; this was agreed verbally. They received electricity supply for over a year until the property was completed, but they turned around and refused to build the wall as the verbal agreement was broken.

Arif got a solicitor who wrote letters to Mr Khan, asking him to pay for the electricity. Mr Khan did not respond. Instead, he and his workers assaulted Arif. Arif was about to get into his car that was parked in his own drive when suddenly Mr Khan pulled him out of the car and threw him on the floor, kicking him in the face, eyes, mouth, and even his ankle. Arif, shocked, tried to stand up, but Khan kept on kicking him; he also strangled Arif. Khan left him half dead and called the police. When the police came, Khan lied that Arif had attacked him and made up a story; there was no witness and poor Arif stood up shocked, limping. He called Fatema on the phone who was in a supermarket. She rushed home and saw Arif's face all bruised black and swollen; he could not see through his swollen eyes and his ankle was swollen. Mum said he had to go to the hospital. Arif refused and said, "I am alright." He was trying to be a macho to show he was strong, but Fatema insisted, so he agreed.

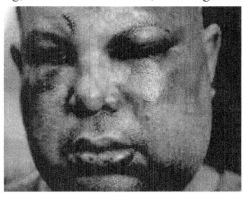

At Heartland Hospital, the nurse put eye drops in his eyes. There were strangle marks around his throat, his swollen ankle needed to be X-rayed and plastered, but Arif refused treatment. He said he wanted to go home as he was very tired and weak, the waiting time was very long. The hospital report read, "There were strangle marks around his neck, his ankle, eyes, and face bruised and swollen, patient declined treatment."

Fatema gave Arif some painkillers before he went to sleep; she prayed for him and was very worried as his injuries were visibly painful.

Shiraz was in the house when Arif was being beaten up; he came out when the police arrived. He spoke in the neighbour's favour, saying Arif went to the neighbour's place. Fatema told the police Shiraz was lying, that he was inside the house and could not have seen what happened, Arif was beaten up in his own drive. The police chose to listen to the liar because, as per Fatima's guess, Shiraz is an old man.

Fatema was looking for a place to move out of the house; Arif found a two-bedroom retirement apartment nearby, and together, they moved out of their home. Shiraz was no longer his nearest relative. Under the Mental Health Act, the nearest relative is not the same as the next of kin. The next of kin have no rights under the Mental Health Act. Your nearest relative is the oldest person in your home by age, and they can ask for an assessment to decide if you should be detained in a hospital. Your nearest relative can apply to discharge you from the mental health treatment. Shiraz did not understand Arif had done nothing wrong. All Shiraz wanted was free treatment.

Shiraz is very crafty, sly and deceitful. He went to his GP again and arranged for someone to see his son, Arif, as, according to him, he felt that he was depressed and needed treatment. He told the GP that he was violent and was involved in a fight with the neighbours. Shiraz also told Arif that he would receive free treatment and many other facilities free of charge, and he will also claim 'job seeker's/disability allowance. Police and social workers never stopped knocking at Fatema's door, asking for Arif. Either he was not in, or he told them to go and never come back.

Finally, all six police officers, a social worker and a psychiatrist came with a warrant for Arif's arrest. Fatema was shocked. She pleaded to Shiraz, "Please, leave him alone. Don't do this; there's absolutely nothing wrong with him." But Shiraz, in a very low voice, whispered, "I'll show you who his nearest relative or next of kin is."

Fatema said, "May Lord God punish you."

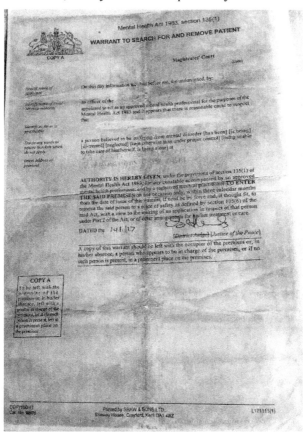

Shiraz signed the agreement papers for Arif to be removed from the home. Fatema saw him sign it. A copy was given to Shiraz, who hid the papers, and he lied to Arif that his mum signed the papers. Both Arif and Amana did not see it as they were talking to the people around them.

Arif said, "Mum, don't worry, I'll be back soon!" Fatema prayed hard for him, but he was not back. Two days later, he phoned from a payphone, saying, "Mum, can you phone back? This is a payphone; they have taken my mobile phone and everything from me." It was his new latest phone, and he was concerned that it would not be returned to him. Fatema phoned him back; Arif explained to her that they were giving him good food, three meals a day, all freshly cooked. He told her the visiting hours and asked her to bring clothes, socks, sleepers, a nail cutter, toothbrush, toothpaste, and a prayer mat.

Fatema washed and ironed Arif's clothes, packed all requested items, and visited him with a full suitcase. It was a beautiful new five-star hospital; Arif came out of his room, and two security guards followed him. They all went into the office. Arif was given his mobile phone, his wallet, and all the things that were taken from him. He was relieved to see his phone was not damaged. Then, he was escorted to the waiting room where Fatema was waiting for him. The two guards followed him and were alert listening, so Fatema asked him to speak in Asian 'Kachchhi.' Arif was not very good at his mother tongue, but in a mixed language, he said, "Watch out, dad will kill you.' Fatema said she knew it. "He's got a lot of money; he will pay someone to kill," Arif said again.

Fatema said to Arif that his father was too miser to pay anyone, and that she was wearing the *ta'wiz* to protect herself. She agreed to live in her retirement flat, anyway.

Arif's phone was not charged, so he could not use it. Fatema was to bring his charger next visit. Fatema inquired about his *ta'wiz* and Arif said they opened it and wanted to know what was written in the *ta'wiz*. They thought it was terrorists' code writing. When the visiting time was over, Arif's phone was taken away from him, and he was told he would be allowed to use it only while supervised by guards. No external communication was allowed. Fatema went with him to the office and told the nurse we all wear this religious thing called *ta'wiz*, the amulet for protection. She said it had Arabic verses from the holy book Quran.

Next visit, Fatema took a copy of the Quran with translation and gave it to Arif to keep it near him and read it; she advised him to enjoy the holiday as the new QE Hospital was a five-star hospital. There was a sports room with snooker/table tennis and lots of exercise/fitness facilities for inpatients.

There were morning and afternoon visiting hours. Shiraz visited Arif in the morning, while Fatema visited in the afternoons. Everything went well until a nurse told Shiraz that the hospital rules are that all patients receive treatment. Therefore, they would be administrating very low dose 5mg drugs/tablets. Shiraz agreed he wanted free medication, but Fatema said there was nothing wrong with Arif and he should not be given any drugs. She said the drugs had side effects and gave her an online article that she had printed out.

A new study confirms what researchers have been investigating for a decade:

Anticholinergic drugs are linked with cognitive impairment and an increased risk of dementia. Anticholinergics are a class of drugs that include over the counter and prescription medications used to treat allergies and asthma, as well as sleep disorders and depression, Healthline reports. They may also be prescribed for incontinence, gastrointestinal cramps, and muscular spasms, as well as high blood pressure, chronic obstructive pulmonary disease (COPD) and symptoms of Parkinson's disease.

When Fatema got home, she got a call from a social worker, confirming that Arif was fine. Fatema responded that there was nothing wrong with him, that his dad was a sociopath and was trying to kill her to possess the house and a lot of money. The social worker did not say anything. Fatema continued, "You've got the wrong person. It should be the dad, not my son in the psychiatric hospital." Fatema knew she understood and would act on the message conveyed by her.

Chapter 14

Fatema believes that Shiraz is a sociopath, as all the symptoms below describes him.

Nine Signs of a Sociopath

1) **Sociopaths are charming**. Sociopaths tend to attract people who seek guidance or direction.

2) **Sociopaths are more spontaneous**. Their behaviour often seems irrational or extremely risky.

3) **Sociopaths are incapable** of feeling shame, guilt, or remorse. This allows them to betray people, threaten people or harm people without giving it a second thought.

4) **Sociopaths invent outrageous lies** about their experiences. They wildly exaggerate things to the point of absurdity, but when they describe it to you in a storytelling format, for some reason, it sounds believable at the time.

5) **Sociopaths seek to dominate** others and "win" at all costs. They hate to lose any argument or fight and will viciously defend their web of lies at any cost.

6) **Sociopaths tend to be highly intelligent**, but they use their brainpower to deceive others rather than empower them. Their high IQs often makes them dangerous.

Therefore, many of the best-known serial killers were sociopaths.

7) **Sociopaths are incapable of love** and are entirely self-serving. They may feign love or compassion in order to get what they want, but they do not actually love.

8) **Sociopaths speak poetically.** They are master wordsmiths, able to deliver a running "stream of consciousness" monologue that is both intriguing and hypnotic.

9) **Sociopaths never apologise**. They are never wrong. They never feel guilt.

Psychopath and sociopath are often used interchangeably; since sociopath is not officially diagnosed, there is no clinical difference between the two and cannot be treated with medication. Healthcare providers often use psychotherapy (talk therapy) and medication to treat other mental health conditions such as anxiety, depression, or aggression.

There is no cure for psychopathy. No pill can instill empathy, no vaccine can prevent murder in cold blood, and no amount of talk therapy can change an uncaring mind. For all intents and purposes, psychopaths are lost to the normal social world.

Psychology researchers generally believe that psychopaths tend to be born with the trait. It's likely to be a genetic predisposition, while sociopaths tend to be made by their environment (which is not to say that psychopaths may not also suffer from some sort of childhood trauma).

Dr Kent Kiehl, a psychologist at the University of Mexico and one of the foremost experts on psychopathy, said that the stunted paralimbic system is present from birth.

For psychopaths, who give little thought to punishment rarely, if ever, learn from it. Punishment doesn't discourage their criminality; it cements it. Indeed, psychopaths are six times more likely than other criminals to commit new crimes following release from prison.

Shiraz has all the symptoms of a sociopath; he has no conscience and gets what he wanted at others' expense. He got free medication and free accommodation in a beautiful new five-star hospital. He phoned all his brothers to tell them how clever he was.

Arif was in the five-star psychiatric hospital; he had a solicitor who represented him in several tribunal hearings. He was not forced to take medication.

Fatema had several meetings with psychiatrists and nurses. She spoke to Dr Khan and Dr Loizou; she explained that Arif had never suffered from schizophrenia or any mental illness and that throughout childhood, he had never been psychologically or physically ill, not even minor colds or coughs. She wrote several letters to them and to the

172

solicitor who represented Arif. She wrote, "I as a mother would be worried and seek help if there was anything wrong with my son." She showed them letters that she herself had received from Loizou about her own mental condition. Fatema was present in the tribunal hearings.

Eventually, Arif was discharged from the hospital. His career and job prospects were ruined, though. He was referred to a psychiatrist in every job interview he went to. Although they confirmed that Arif was no longer on medication, it was difficult to get jobs.

When one door closes, God opens another door.

Fatema remembered a saying:

"Sometimes we feel that all doors are closed in our life

But all closed doors may not be locked.

They may be waiting for a gentle push…

*And that is **prayers**."*

Another one says:

"Look on every exit as being an entrance somewhere else."

— Tom Stoppard, Rosencrantz and Guildenstern

19 August 2013

Dear Sir or Madam

Re: Nearest Relative Discharge

I refer to your letter dated 14th August 2013 regarding my son, ⬚⬚⬚⬚⬚ ⬚⬚⬚⬚⬚⬚li, saying that his community treatment has been extended till 23 January 2014. I would like to bring some matters to your attention regarding his supervised community treatment.

⬚⬚⬚ ⬚⬚⬚⬚⬚ had an appointment with Dr Loizou on Friday 5th July 2013. He rang the receptionist on Monday 1st July to the Warstock Lane Centre to request an alternative appointment as he was travelling with a group by coach to Paris on Friday 5th July. (The letter with the Birmingham and Solihull heading dated 3 May 2013, states that "if you are unable to attend the appointment please let us know so we can use the time to see someone else. We will be happy to arrange another date and time for you."

Dr Loizou returned the call saying that he can't cancel the date and threatened him that if he did not attend on that particular day, he will be taken back to the Oleaster Centre. After a long conversation she agreed to refer him to see the CPN and a social worker on the same day (Monday 1st July). He was also given a letter saying that he will have to keep all appointments in future.

⬚⬚⬚ ⬚⬚⬚⬚ is having side effects from the clopixol injections, tremor in hands, dizziness and feeling sleepy most of the time. He applied for a SIA badge and the SIA wrote to Dr Loizou and unfortunately his licence was rejected for the reasons given by her. So my son, ⬚⬚⬚⬚ ⬚ can't get any job like stewarding at cricket and football matches. Warstock Lane are also not very helpful.

Considering all this, I have no other option but to request that ⬚⬚⬚ ⬚⬚⬚ be discharged from Section 17A and from all sections so that he can start living a normal life again.

Yours faithfully

Arif has a place of his own; when he purchased his property, Arif said to Fatema, "I have put your name as the next of kin." Fatema said it was okay, but Shiraz was livid. When Arif was not around, Shiraz started swearing at Fatema and even hit her. Fatema told Arif to not talk about anything in his presence going forward.

Arif later became self-employed. He got married during COVID restrictions with only a handful of guests present; Fatema was present at the wedding ceremony and signed documents as next of kin and as a witness to the matrimonial service at the mosque registration office in Dar-E-Salaam,

174

Tanzania. They enjoyed their stay in a hotel there; it was sunny and warm, and they went to the beautiful sandy beach in Dar. Arif hired a taxi, and they visited relatives in Morogoro. Life in Dar is very much like life that was in Uganda before Idi Amin's expulsion of Asians. Everyone has maids/servants to do the house chores. People are more relaxed.

When Amana got married, Shiraz insisted on having an Islamic sermon recited. He arranged for a Muslim preacher to recite the sermon, but he never paid a penny to him, Amana paid the priest. Fatema's daughters and son got married Shiraz was invited, but he did not attend and did not give a penny in wedding presents; all their children paid for their own wedding expenses.

He never saw Fatema's only grandson and never sent a penny to him. He does not even acknowledge him as his relative.

Fatema wants to sell her property as for the past 30 years she has been paying the mortgage, insurance, and everything. She has all the court documents authorising her to sell the property. The cleaning process is going slowly as Shiraz wants to sort out the abundant rubbish that he has collected over the years. The other reason is that there was a burst pipe in the house and the whole ceiling collapsed, making everything soaking wet. In order to have repair work carried out, Shiraz managed to remove some of his rubbish that he put outside in the back patio and covered it with plastic sheets. It's like a mountain of rubbish in the back veranda/garden; it may take years to clear it.

The works after the burst pipe are now completed. The pipes are fixed, Fatema got a new bathroom done, and ceiling plastered. Now, all walls need painting; once everything is done, Fatema will get an estate agent to value the property. Due to COVID lockdown restrictions, the work has been delayed. Some of the rubbish has to be taken to the recycling, but Shiraz is taking advantage of restrictions and is deliberately delaying the clearing process. All the rubbish that he has collected need to be thrown out.

3. UPON the respondent husband having signed letters of authority for disclosure of any information relating to any accounts, shares, bonds, ISAs, pensions, and any other investments held by him

IT IS ORDERED BY CONSENT that:

4. Sale of the Former Matrimonial Home

   a. The order of District Judge Williams of 13 May 2013 is varied to allow the applicant wife to have sole conduct of the sale of the Former Matrimonial Home.

The order is varied to allow the wife to have sole conduct of the Former Matrimonial Home.

IT IS ORDERED

1. Mr ⬚ shall by 4pm 31st January 2018 give possession of ⬚ ⬚ to Mrs ⬚ so that she may effect a sale of the property.

2. For the removal of doubt Mrs ⬚ may issue a warrant for possession on or after 1st February 2018 if Mr ⬚ does not comply with paragraph 1 of this order.

3. Nothing in this order shall prevent Mr ⬚ from buying out Mrs ⬚ share in the property before 31st January 2018 if he is able to do so.

For removal of doubt, Mrs to issue a warrant for possession of the property.

Sale of 23 ⬚

As per the court order dated 27 May 2016, one of the two ⬚ ⬚ ⬚ and your husband concerns the sale, or lack of sale, of 2⬚ has no co-operated over the sale of particular, it refers to your concerns that your husband ⬚ 'such a mess that it is the property and that agents have advised that the property is in 'such a mess that it is unlikely that it is marketable in its current condition'.

It would be very helpful if we had a statement from the agents setting out the above.

Would you please be able to provide me with the details of the agent and firm who cam⬚ view the property and who stated this please? I will then contact them to see if they c⬚ his in writing.

⬚ook forward to hearing from you.

The agents have advised the property is in such a mess that it is unlikely to be marketable in current condition.

c. The mess in the house is ⬚
purchasers.

18. As to why she should not be bound by that agreement she stated:
   a. Mr ⬚ has expressed a wish to buy her out – and she will accept any reasonable offer for her 60% share.
   b. Mr ⬚ will not keep the house clean.
   c. She did not say that he could live in the house indefinitely.
   d. There is continued non disclosure of cash assets.

19. At the hearing on 29th March 2017 she complained that Mr ⬚ keeps swearing at her and has threatened to kill her which he appeared to deny. There is an issue between them over Muhammed who is currently detained in a mental hospital as a result of Mr ⬚ procuring the issue of a warrant for his removal from the home under Section 135 Mental Health Act 1983. I was told that Muhammed will be discharged from hospital shortly and will be returning to 23 Robin Hood Crescent. Mrs ⬚ said that if the house was sold then Mu⬚ can live with her. ⬚ ⬚'s condition and there is no

Shiraz keeps swearing and has threatened to kill Fatema.

177

The second question is whether it is ~~~~~ entirely in his favour and ~~~
consideration – it is an agreement which operates entirely in his favour and ~~~
unwelcome effect of keeping Mrs ..... out of her 60% share for a further period
which is potentially his remaining life span.

24. There is no evidence that Mr .... has changed his position in the legal sense by
relying upon the agreement so that to hold Mrs .... to it would operate unfairly or
unconscionably. On the contrary, the agreement cements the position he has held out
since the order was agreed, namely that he stays in the property at Mrs .
expense. .... her agreement in October 2016 and that

Mr stays in the property at Mrs' expense.

Robin Hood Crescent ....
sale notwithstanding that he had agreed to it in the consent order of May 2013. As a
result of his lack of co-operation I varied the directions as to sale in my order dated 19th
August 2016 to give Mrs .... 'i sole conduct of the sale. She duly instructed Agents to
undertake a market appraisal.

14. Their advice is that the property is currently unmarketable due to the house being filled
with rubbish in black bin liners. I have been provided with photographs which confirm
the position and in the light of them I am not surprised at the agent's advice. I note that
this point is referred to in the petition as part of the allegations of behaviour against Mr
Mahrali so I infer that this has been a state of affairs going back some considerable time.

Court order has enabled Fatema to have sole conduct of
the sale of the property.

Fatema tried to clean the house and called estate agents
to have it valued. Shiraz neither wants to move out nor wants
to buy out Fatema's share. He says he will not give a penny
of 'his' money. The agents have advised Fatema the property
is in such a mess, she may have to auction it. They cannot
market it in such a condition; it must be to a saleable standard
to market it, which will also increase its value.

27. Accordingly the order should prevail. I will adjourn this part of the application
    period of 8 weeks to enable Mr   to raise funds to buy out Mrs   If no
    progress can be made on that score then he should understand that if there is continued
    non co – operation in relation to a sale I will be considering very seriously making an
    order that he gives possession of the property to Mrs   so that she can arrange the
    clearance of the rubbish in the house, its cleaning and subsequent marketing and sale. Mr
    .   has other assets and he will not be financially embarrassed by having to make
    arrangements to rent a temporary home pending the sale of the property.

8. As this judgment was reserved it will have to be the subject of formal hand down in open
   court for which a hearing notice is attached. Both parties are excused from attending that
   hearing.

6th April 2017

Judge Musgrave

:ham Civil and Family Justice Centre

Divorcing such a violent person was the best thing Fatema has ever done. Arif, her son, supports her in this matter. She wishes she had done it earlier in her life; it would have saved all the suffering for both Arif and her.

***

Fatema remembers watching Amazing Chimpanzee' A Documentary film directed by Pierre Stine, released in 2012.[3]

After humans, chimpanzees are the most intelligent of our planet's primates, and they've developed impressive ways of communicating. These clever critters "talk" to each other using different gestures, facial expressions, and numerous vocalisations, too, such as hoots, grunts, and screams.

---

[3] Movieclips Trailers. (2012, April 17). *Chimpanzee Official Trailer #1 (2012) Disney Nature Movie HD* [Video]. YouTube. https://www.youtube.com/watch?v=KokQL4aLfrI&list=PLJ8v7JiEPp HLjnVHsQHwFSQj4sgI5uW-d&index=4

The film shows how in the wilderness, a male chimpanzee nicknamed Freddy adopts an orphan baby chimpanzee called Oscar and brings him up as his own. It's an amazing true story. The narrator said that in all his life, he had never encountered a male animal adopting a baby. Oscar would have died in the wilderness had he not been adopted by Freddy.

Fatema told Arif to ask Shiraz to watch the documentary film, but he did not agree. She told Amana even animals are better than him; they feed not only their own children but also adopt other orphan baby animals.

Statement of Truth

I declare that the contents of this statement are true and placed before the court in evidence.

Printed in Great Britain
by Amazon

79740667R00108